The Seven Secrets of Influence

The Seven Secrets of Influence

Elaina Zuker

McGraw-Hill, Inc.

New York   St. Louis   San Francisco   Auckland   Bogotá
Caracas   Hamburg   Lisbon   London   Madrid
Mexico   Milan   Montreal   New Delhi   Paris
San Juan   São Paulo   Singapore
Sydney   Tokyo   Toronto

Library of Congress Cataloging-in-Publication Data

Zuker, Elaina.
    The seven secrets of influence / Elaina Zuker.
        p.   cm.
    Includes index.
    ISBN 0-07-073085-7
    1. Influence (Psychology)   2. Persuasion (Psychology)   3. Success—
Psychological aspects.   I. Title.   II. Title: Seven secrets of
influence.
BF774.Z84   1991
153.8'52—dc20   91-16189
                                                            CIP

1 2 3 4 5 6 7 8 9 0   DOC/DOC   9 7 6 5 4 3 2 1

ISBN   0-07-073085-7

*The sponsoring editor for this book was James H. Bessent, Jr., the editing
supervisor was Marion B. Castellucci, and the production supervisor was
Donald Schmidt. This book was set in Baskerville. It was composed by
McGraw-Hill's Professional Book Group composition unit.*

Printed and bound by R. R. Donnelley & Sons Company.

To Sarah and Louis Zuker, and Shirley and Oscar, whose gentle and powerful influence lives on

Contents

17. The Magic of Rapport: Setting the Stage for Greater Influence   188

Preface

In the back room of my office suite, there is a large three-drawer vertical file cabinet labeled "Influence." Its monstrous stacked drawers reach almost to my waist and measure about 2½ feet wide and about 16 inches deep.

Inside, elbowing each other for breathing room, are hundreds of file folders—containing thousands of papers—many old and worn, some new and bright yellow, green, red, or purple. They bear identifying labels like "Research," "Clients," "Questionnaires," "Training Programs," "Speaking Engagements," "Customer Feedback," "Evaluations and Kudos," "Influence Skills for Technical Professionals," "Influence Skills for Managers," "Influence Skills for Salespeople," "Book Proposals— Drafts 1 through 9," "Audio Tape Course—Scripts for 6-Hour Version; 2-Hour Version; 1-Hour Program." There are four huge files called "Articles" and another one titled "Miscellaneous."

The contents of these drawers, and this book, are the result of my work on this subject for over ten years. I still find it hard to believe (and most satisfying) that all the research, thinking, writing, speaking, presenting, listening, fine-tuning, and rewriting of all those years and those thousands of papers are now distilled into a (relatively) slim volume, this book called *The Seven Secrets of Influence*.

The idea for this book came from a seminar I created and conducted with groups of managers and professionals in corporations all over America. It's based on real work with real people who need real hands-on skills to help them in their daily interactions, as they attempt to work together in the increasingly tough and competitive environments of most organizations today.

In 1979 I was a professor of management in the department of business at Montclair State College, and I also had a small practice as a consultant in organizational development and management training. One of my clients, AT&T, which employed thousands of technical professionals—physicists, data processors, telecommunications specialists—needed help. While these individuals were extraordinarily competent in their technical or professional skills—indeed, AT&T and Bell Labs had the largest number of Nobel Prize winners in-house—they lacked the interpersonal and influence skills to work in teams, to interact with others from other disciplines, and to "sell" their ideas and projects to upper management.

I had been in sales and sales management all my life (having been successful selling encyclopedias to families, advertising space to apparel manufacturers, and public relations projects to *Fortune* 500 corporations, and having managed a staff of sales people). My challenge now was to take what I had learned about successful selling to *outside* customers and adapt it so it could be used by people who didn't think of themselves as salespeople to sell "inside" their companies.

With a team of organizational psychologists, I did some research, interviewing the people in different groups and departments, and developed a three-day off-site meeting to help with these issues. It was an almost instant hit—these "techies" were eager to learn all they could to become more skillful in their relationships with coworkers, bosses, and subordinates.

We discovered that this was a neglected group at AT&T and most other organizations insofar as training and development were concerned. Most training programs were directed at managers or executives. The training that *was* offered to professionals and "individual contributors" was usually informational, intended to help them further develop their technical skills.

What began as an off-site meeting evolved into a more structured seminar. We called it "Mastering Influence Skills."

AT&T began offering our program in their training catalog for various population groups: first for members of the technical staff, then for managers and supervisors, then for sales and marketing people. The program continued to be offered to sold-out groups and excellent ratings. Other Bell Systems companies—AT&T International, Bell Labs, Bellcore—joined our client list and offered the program in every training curriculum.

Other corporations became clients: IBM, Bankers Trust, Citibank, Chase Manhattan. Each had a specific need or a special population group that needed the benefits of influence skills. American Express was teaching project management to its managers all over the world;

what they needed to complete their proficiency in managing and completing projects was the missing skill—influence skill. Amex now teaches the Mastering Influence Skills program in five languages to its project managers.

MCI cleverly titled the program "Mastering Influence Skills for Technical Information Communication" (MISTIC) and offered it in their technical training curriculum. Sheraton Corporation had just instituted a quality service program, but its managers needed influence skills to motivate their employees in all the hotels to actively use and support the customer service effort.

As our client group widened, it was no longer possible for our small internal staff to give the program to hundreds (and then thousands) of people in corporations. We developed a "train the trainer" system. This system involved restructuring the program, creating discrete and reproducible modules, and developing a complete trainers/leaders' guide, so that in-house trainers (from Citibank, Borg-Warner, IBM, L'Oreal Cosmetics, and so on) could learn the program, and then learn how to teach it, on their own, to their hundreds of internal "customers."

We have now taught the program to thousands of people, either via in-house trainers or our own staff consultants and trainers in many corporations and organizations all over the United States and Canada. We continue to fine-tune the program based on changes we see in the corporate environment, the business world, the economy, and—most important—on feedback and conversations we have with our ultimate customer and end-user, that individual manager, professional, or salesperson who needs the skills our program can offer.

We continue to do research, formally and informally. To me, each new client, participant, and reader is a research population of one. I want to know all I can about *you*—your job, your goals, and your challenges, issues, and concerns. What skills will help you be more successful in your business relationships?

In this way, I would like you to consider this book a conversation, a dialogue, between us, in which I am sharing with you the results of my conversations and experiences with many others—some like you and some very different from you. All, though, have one thing in common: we want to be more effective, more potent, and more satisfied in our day-to-day lives. I hope that this book helps you toward that goal. And in the spirit of conversation and ongoing dialogue, I would welcome your comments, your knowledge, and your success stories.

Acknowledgments

It is somehow fitting that, as I sit down to write this, it's Academy Awards day. Like almost everyone else I know, I sit glued to the set for hours, through the numbing presentations ceremony. I always muse and wonder, how will this person handle his or her acceptance speech? Will she do the usual, "No project is done alone—this was a team effort. I want to thank my Aunt Millie, my first acting coach, the Director, etc.?"

Whenever I begin reading a book, I always turn to the acknowledgments to see who was the "team" behind the scenes, who helped the author through the thorny times, the "stuck" spots, and the obstacles (like the "team" described by Kurt Vonnegut in *Cat's Cradle*). When a friend writes a book, I quickly turn to the acknowledgments page to see if my name is on it.

Now that I'm faced with the task, I have had to reflect on the process of writing this book, from its inception to final production. And try as I will to be unique and different, I must, alas, conform to the same approach as all the others.

First, my profound thanks to my agent (spelled "angel"), Bob Silverstein, of Quicksilver Books, who shepherded this project through its many incarnations, helping me to shape the initial proposal into a clear and appealing one and then navigating it through the labyrinth of the publishing world, until he found a good, secure, and understanding home for it at McGraw-Hill.

When one works with corporations in the role of consultant (or writer), most often the transaction is pretty straightforward. You have something they want—they entertain bids for similar products or services—and then they choose one based on quality, price, or some other criterion. In this case, you're a *vendor*.

Sometimes the process is a little warmer than this—you have a unique service or you develop a special relationship and the resulting work is more of a collaborative effort. Now, you're a *consultant*.

But every once in a great while, you encounter people who see the artistry—in the program, the product, the service, in you. They see the "fit" with the needs in their organization. Most important, they have the vision, courage, and *influence skills* to take a stand and stretch the limits of the tried-and-true. They function like impresarios or patrons, and they help me be an *artist*. When this occurs, it's more like making music than like work. The distinguished members of my Client Hall of Fame are: Marge Stockhammer of AT&T, Ron Koprowski of Chase Manhattan, Dan White of Citibank, Linda Barker and Melinda Bickerstaff of American Express, Linda Collier and Maribeth Kirby of Bellcore, Nan Palmer of Sheraton Corp., Sarah Townsend of Borg-Warner, Isabel Kerson of L'Oreal, and the latest champion, Eloise Glasgall of MCI.

A special thanks to a special person, and my idea of a great professional, for his wisdom, caring, and generous advice. Buck Blessing lives up to his name, and has bestowed many blessings on me, helping me to make quantum leaps and realize the magic of leverage. Seeing the larger national potential of the influence training program was a key ingredient in my motivation, commitment, and scope of the book.

My thanks to Dr. William Vingiano for his assistance early in the development of the Influence Styles Inventory and to Dr. Richard Altschuler for his help in the analysis of my research data and in the writing of the appendix.

The input, suggestions, and professional expertise of Leslie Rosen were especially valuable in the creation of the Train-the-Trainers program.

Thanks to Jonathan Cohen, for his eloquence, clarity, and patience in helping with both the "architecture" and the "bricklaying." Thanks, too, to Maura Christopher for technical suggestions in the early stages of the manuscript.

My sincere appreciation goes to the dedicated professionals who have worked by my side and helped to deliver the Mastering Influence Skills program to corporate clients in a fashion that has done me proud: Cheryl Hepburn Greenhalgh, Carol Sage, Linda de Carlo. Thanks to them, too, and to Maryann Giarratano, for their energy and expertise in helping to make our showcases so successful, and for being a team of supporters I can always count on.

A special thanks goes to the gang at Day-Timers, with Bob Dorney at the top of the list. He wins the Oscar, hands down, for vision, courage, and influence. He saw the potential in the seedling of an idea and helped me realize a long-held dream—*The Seven Secrets of Influence* as a six-cassette audio program, packaged and marketed worldwide by

Day-Timers. Seeing the marketability of the program gave me (and the publishing world) the confidence to adapt this material as a book. Thanks also to Mark Ladouceur, Steve Rowley, and especially to Mary Ellen South, my friend and fellow adventurer.

In a category by herself is L. J. Herman, who understands this program (and the book) almost better than I do, and whose brilliant words have helped to advertise the tape, the showcase, and my speeches and seminars.

Thanks, too, to Stewart Wolpin and Howard Blumenthal, whose assistance with the audio scripts helped make the writing of the book so much smoother. And Sonya Schwartz's masterful handling of an often confusing array of diskettes, progressive drafts, and illegible notes helped to make a clear manuscript.

Helpers early on, but not forgotten: Allyn Finly and Jim Wall, for their design expertise; Arthur Domingo for his help with shaping the essence of Mastering Influence Skills to the press.

Special mentions: Joan Alevras, whose early influence, support, and brilliance had a profound impact on all my consulting and writing work; Alexandria Hatcher, who first believed in this book and began the process of bringing it to the publishing community; Carole Hyatt, whose example, friendship, and advice have been invaluable; Frank Hertle, for his help as a poet in developing my "rhyming" influence styles; and Dorothy Hertle, for introducing me to Bill Wilson, without whose guidance I might not have been here to write this book.

On a personal note, I am most grateful to my loving and patient friends and family, who have had to listen to and learn more about influence than they ever wanted to know, and who comforted and propped me up during all the years of struggles and rejections. Particularly, to my dear Nancy Vaughn Miller, whose feedback, suggestions, and marketing genius helped give birth to the title.

And finally, my sincere thanks to the thousands of men and women who have attended our seminars, workshops, conferences, and speeches, who came as students and ended up being my teachers.

They all contributed so generously of their time, their attention, and their insights, feedback, challenges, questions, suggestions, and ideas. Without them, I would still be teaching and writing about the same ideas I started with, ten years ago. With them, I have been enriched, enlightened, and emboldened to explore new areas and expand my body of work. And that has made all the difference.

Elaina Zuker

PART 1

You May Be Closer to Influence Than You Think

There are 12 things I want this book to do for you. The best way to start is simply to spell out the benefits I think you will derive from this program.

1. *The 7 Secrets of Influence will help you identify your individual styles of influence.*

In Chapter 4 there is a questionnaire that will give you insight into your own influence style or influence strategy. You may not even be aware that you are using a particular strategy. It's likely you are subconsciously automatically, or naturally using a combination of strategies in your everyday dealings with people.

2. *You'll learn to establish rapport using verbal and nonverbal techniques.*

Rapport is usually described as a feeling of trust and comfort when you're dealing with someone. You'll learn some easy and dramatic ways to establish rapport with others.

3. *You'll learn how people process information.*

Many of you, especially in technical fields, have a good idea about how computers process information. Humans are simply more sophisticated information processors, albeit a little less organized.

But unlike machines, we all process information differently. If you can tune in to the information processing strategies different people use, you can become a more powerful influencer.

4. *You'll learn to elicit high-quality, precise information.*

How much you can influence someone is completely dependent on how precise and complete the information is that you get from them.

5. *You'll learn refined listening skills.*

Refined listening skills is another way of saying finely tuned attentiveness. Listening is a key skill used in influencing. But there are many ways to listen, and *The 7 Secrets* covers the ones that lead to increased influence.

6. *You'll understand other people's decision making strategies.*

The way people make decisions varies as greatly as their ways of processing information. How people make decisions is detectable, and you'll learn how to detect these processes.

7. *You'll enhance your ability to facilitate other people's decisions.*

In addition to identifying decision making strategies, you will also practice skills that help you help others reach decisions so that both of you get what you want.

8. *You'll package your communication to fit specific situations and people.*

A key skill in influencing people is to package your ideas in forms that people will react to positively. But make no mistake. Packaging your proposals or ideas is much more than just simply telling people what they want to hear.

9. *You'll have a more flexible behavioral repertoire.*

We'll examine discrete behavioral strategies to influence different types of people. You'll have many opportunities to practice and develop a variety of strategies that will eventually become integrated into your everyday intuitive behavior patterns.

10. *You'll produce effective solutions by influencing the decisions and behaviors of others.*

Being able simply to influence one individual often isn't enough. You'll learn how to help groups come to agreement.

11. *You'll gain credibility and enlist support.*

The best way to influence is to gain credibility—to get people to trust you and support your ideas.

12. *You'll be thorough, competent, and forceful—winningly, skillfully, and gracefully.*

Influence can be an art as well as a skill, something that can be elegant and graceful. You'll learn that one of the most important influence skills is actually the art of keeping your influence invisible.

1

Influence— Getting What You Want

Influence. Everyone wants it. But how do you get it? Like the weather, influence is usually noticed only by its outcome. When you've changed someone's mind or opinion, you notice the change. But the methods or strategies you used are usually instinctive. You often aren't sure of exactly what you did that worked.

Since we generally aren't aware of how we influence other people, it's easy to believe that this ability is a mysterious gift or talent. You either have it, or you don't have it. Or, you may believe that influence is a privilege exercised only by those who already wield power.

But anyone can have influence. Influence is a set of interpersonal skills that can be learned, practiced, and mastered.

When I became aware that people view influence as a desirable, but elusive, quality, I developed a unique method for identifying influence as a set of skills and began teaching it in a workshop setting. I've conducted hundreds of these workshops and through them have taught thousands of people how to perfect and hone their influence skills.

This book is the essence of the workshops. In it you will learn how to assess your own influence style and how to use a formula for influencing others in your professional and personal life. In this first chapter, I set the foundation by helping you discover what true influence is and what it isn't.

What Pushes Your Buttons?

To learn how to influence others, you start by understanding how you yourself are influenced. Here's a self-awareness exercise that will help you do that.

A note on the exercises for those of you whose parents or teachers told them never to write in a book! This book is different. It's intended to be a personal, hands-on learning experience—a workbook and reference manual. So feel free to write in the spaces provided. That's why they're there.

Influence Exercise 1: What Influences You?

It's easy to see influence as a process if you think of a personal situation. In Exercise 1 you're asked to try to think of a time when you were influenced, when someone was able to change your opinion, attitude, or behavior. Maybe a teacher helped you meet a special challenge, or a friend convinced you to buy one car rather than another.

Try to recall what that person said or did to influence you. What triggers or "hot buttons" of yours were pushed? Were you offered a reward? Was logic used? Or were you painted a brighter vision of the future? What words or phrases influenced you? Spend a few minutes to visualize the situation, to recall the verbal and nonverbal communication. Close your eyes and replay the scene in your mind. Write down your answers in the space provided for Exercise 1.

Influence Exercise 2: Influence Factors Checklist

For instance, power may be something that influenced you. Or, you may have been influenced by the chance to fulfill a goal. Exercise 2 is a list of influence factors that can help you understand what influences you. But remember that each of us is influenced in different ways. What influences you may not be on the list. And what influences you one day may not appeal to you the next. Since the goal of these first exercises is for you to begin to discover what influences you, do the best you can with the clues provided to trigger your memory.

Influence Exercise 1: What Influences You?

As you remember a time when you were influenced, try to capture the key components or elements of what that person said or did. Did he or she offer you a reward? Use logic? Paint a brighter vision of the future? What words or phrases influenced you? Write down as many of them as you can think of.

1. The person who influenced me was: _____

_____

_____

2. I was influenced to (do, think, change, believe): _____

_____

_____

3. The key reasons I was influenced were (for example, to maintain the status quo, to face reality, to take the practical course, to accept the person's future vision, financial reward, fear of loss, prospect of good relationship, etc.): _____

_____

_____

_____

_____

4. The words and phrases that influenced me were: _____

_____

_____

_____

_____

_____

Influence Exercise 2: Influence Factors Checklist

Below is a list of values or tendencies that many people say are the kinds of things that influence them. Completing this list will help you understand what influences you. You may also realize you are influenced by things not on this list.

I am influenced by:	Yes	No
Those I trust	___	___
Good rapport	___	___
Logic, data, or analysis	___	___
An appeal to my intuition	___	___
Authority or power in another person	___	___
The chance to use my own power and authority	___	___
Money	___	___
Anger	___	___
Rewards	___	___
Threats	___	___
Maintaining the status quo	___	___
A consensus among others	___	___
The chance to be happy	___	___
Thrill or risk-taking	___	___
A sense of security	___	___
The chance to achieve	___	___
Competence or efficiency	___	___
Adventure	___	___
Friendship	___	___
Creativity	___	___
Moral or ethical arguments	___	___
The chance to help others or help society	___	___
Recognition	___	___

Independence   —— ——

Practical considerations   —— ——

The chance to benefit   —— ——

Other (please specify): _____

_____

_____

Influence Exercise 3:
You as Influencer

In Exercise 1, you may have found it easy to think of instances when you were influenced. Did the other person's influence over you seem to be more of a strategic process or a random series of arguments? Just as often you are an *influencer*. To see for yourself, try Influence Exercise 3.

Think about a time when *you* influenced someone. Maybe you talked someone into changing jobs, or maybe you simply convinced someone to try out a new place for lunch. Again, try to visualize the verbal and nonverbal exchange. Write down what happened in the space provided.

You can probably think of one or two things you said that really turned the other person around. But those easily remembered moments were the culmination of a longer sequence of events. If you could break situations down into a distinct sequence of events and then dissect

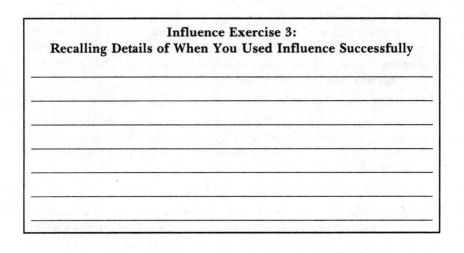

Influence Exercise 3:
Recalling Details of When You Used Influence Successfully

those events into small, observable bits — and you could remember those bits — you could incorporate them into your behavior. In a sense, you could call this the "technology" of influence. And with enough practice you could strategically repeat those bits whenever you needed to influence someone. That is what you'll learn to do throughout this book.

A New Definition of Influence

What Influence Isn't

What exactly do we mean by *influence*? What is this quality that can inspire brilliant performance and motivate people? There are a lot of misconceptions about what influence is and what it isn't. One is that *influence* and *power* are synonymous. Power is certainly a form of influence, but it's often the least effective. That's because when a person relies on power alone to get results, in the long run others are unlikely to cooperate willingly and mutually beneficial relationships are unlike to form.

Let's examine some common myths and misconceptions about influence.

Misconception: The most visible or vocal person is the most influential.

Reality: Often, the person who talks the most or is the most visible is not necessarily the most powerful. When people are talking or displaying themselves, their attention is focused inward and they are more likely to miss cues and information about the situation and other people. These are the very cues that are most necessary to influence others.

Misconception: Real managers don't need influence.

Reality: Like real men don't eat quiche? That used to be true, but it isn't anymore, as we'll see. These days, *all* managers need to influence their subordinates more effectively. The old style of "command management" simply doesn't work anymore. This critical change in management will be explored in detail in Chaper 3.

Misconception: Influence is the same as communication.

Reality: Not everything you say and do is geared toward influencing someone. Sometimes we are simply getting along with people. Influence skills are a subset of communication skills used specifically to persuade someone else.

Misconception: Influence is manipulation.

Reality: The question of whether influence is the same as manipulation is important, particularly because some people use the words *influence* and *manipulation* interchangeably. This is not surprising, considering that the dictionary definition of *manipulation* is "skillful handling." Unfortunately, because the word *manipulation* carries such a heavy negative connotation, many people avoid the use of the word *influence*. But influence is not the same as manipulation, and should not be considered evil or immoral. Here's why. *Manipulation* can be best characterized as dishonest, overly aggressive actions designed to cause someone to change his or her belief or behavior to benefit the manipulator. The key word is *dishonest*.

Tuning In to Your Intuition

How's your conscience—either as someone influencing someone else or as the person being influenced? How you feel is probably the best measure of whether influence or manipulation is at work. If as the influencer, your motives are honest and your intention is to benefit the other person, then you are practicing positive influence. Conversely, if you're on the receiving end, do you feel you're being led in a direction you don't want to go, for someone else's benefit? If you feel uncomfortable, then you're being manipulated.

Paying close attention to your feelings may not seem to be the most scientific method of identifying manipulation, but it is often the most effective. For instance, Olivia, the owner of an art gallery in New York City, recently shared a conversation with me that she had with another art dealer.

> I just had a really queasy feeling. She was saying all the right things, about how glad she was about my recent success, and how she supported what I was trying to do. But I just didn't feel right. It felt as if she was leading up to ask me for a favor that I probably wouldn't have considered it she had asked me straight out.

Everyone has intuitive feelings like this, but for some reason, we don't trust them. If you need something more concrete than feelings, look for incongruities or actions that are incompatible with a person's words over a period of time. Does the person always promise but seldom deliver? Do you find yourself continually making excuses for someone else's lack of integrity? Once you sense someone's pattern, you will see when he or she manipulates. Usually, in human interaction in business, *actions speak louder than words*.

Whenever you have instinctual, intuitive feelings like these, trust them. Such feelings often indicate that the other person is being manipulative—and doing it poorly—in a way that inhibits communication. The behavior *seems* positive, but a separate, selfish objective may be lurking beneath the surface. In my friend Olivia's case, the surface behavior—all that praise and blathering about support—seemed positive. But she sensed this was a prelude to the other shoe falling—a favor or a sales pitch. You know the pattern. *That's* manipulation.

Often, when confronted with manipulative behavior, you will feel anxious, pushed around, angry, unnecessarily compliant, or willing to give in. Maybe you will find yourself resisting getting together with the person, having headaches just before an appointment with him, arriving late, or avoiding continuing the relationship.

We have all been victims of manipulators. Even the most shrewd and sophisticated among us have given our trust and goodwill to another and have been taken in. There are times, however, when you are more vulnerable than others; for example, when you're feeling unsure of yourself—when you've started a new job or are in an unfamiliar work situation, when you've moved to a new town or have met a new group of friends. People are also vulnerable to manipulation during periods of low self-esteem. When you don't feel good about yourself, you have less personal power and less ability to perceive and stand up to manipulative attempts. You become, as they say, a potential "soft touch" to a manipulator.

The desire to please others also leaves us open to manipulation. In this regard, women, especially in the business world, are more vulnerable to manipulation than men are. Men, however, are often less sensitive and astute than women are in identifying when they are being manipulated.

Of course, most manipulators get their just desserts: the four Rs. These are:

Resentment on the part of the "victims"

Recrimination in the form of official or unofficial censure by a boss or colleague who learns of the deed, for example

Remorse on the part of the manipulator, who may regret the indirect or dishonest way he or she acted

Revenge by the people who have been manipulated or treated unfairly, in ways that the manipulator often deserves

The moral: Even though a manipulator may get what he or she wants in the short run, in the long run manipulation doesn't pay. There are much more savvy and ethical ways of achieving a goal. Manipulation is a failed attempt at influence.

As you begin to understand, develop, and learn the influence skills in this book, not only will you be able to get what you want *without* manipulating others, but you will be more confident, more skilled, and less vulnerable to others' attempts to manipulate you.

The Gentle Art

So far, we've talked about what influence isn't:

Influence isn't power alone.

Influence isn't just communication.

Influence isn't manipulation.

Influence Exercise 4:
What Influence Means to You

So what is influence? What does *influence* mean to you? Write your definition in the space provided in Exercise 4.

Influence Exercise 4: What Influence Means to You

Write your definition of *influence* here: _____

_____

_____

_____

Now write down what you'd be able to accomplish if you had more influence. How would things be different?

_____

_____

_____

_____

_____

In the seminars I give on influence, I frequently ask participants how they define influence. Here are some of the responses they've given over the years:

"Influence is getting someone to do what you want, without exerting authority."

"Influence is the ability to achieve an end result."

"Influence is getting people to come to an agreement."

"Influence is soliciting the cooperation of others to help you."

"Influence is changing a person's attitudes or behavior."

These are partly accurate definitions that apply only in specific situations. For the purposes of this book, here's a broader, more accurate definition of what I mean by influence.

Influence is the ability to affect others—seen only in its effect—without exertion of force or formal authority.

To understand this definition better, let's examine its parts.

"The Ability to Affect Others..."

This is the *positive* use of power, the potential or capacity of influence. This power is like electricity—it's only effective when you turn it on and put it into action.

"...Seen Only in Its Effect..."

In other words, results, not only methods, count. If you and your actions created a difference, incurred a change, or made an impact, then you had influence. What you did to create that change may not have been noticeable.

"...Without Exertion of Force or Formal Authority"

Influence is a gentle skill, a much more refined approach to affecting others than the use of authority or coercion.

Any bully or power-crazed boss can force you to do something that's against your natural inclination. But the change that results from force will only be short-term, and such behavior breeds distrust and hostility over the long run. It takes *skill* to truly influence for positive, long-term results for both sides.

Dovetailing—Your Win-Win Strategy

Influence is a positive process. You get the results you want while allowing others to get the results they want. It's a mutually beneficial relationship. Your needs and outcomes dovetail with those of the other person. This dovetailing enables you to keep your own personal integrity while respecting the other person's integrity. Although you can't set other people's goals for them, you can help them get what they want while you're getting what you want.

Dovetailing is the smart way to insure your own success. And it's key to understanding positive influencing. Other people become your allies rather than your saboteurs. If people can benefit from their relationship with you, they'll be more likely to help you achieve your goals. This is the most important feature of influence skills— your ability to create a win-win situation. In his illuminating book entitled *Influencing Human Behavior*, Harry Overstreet reinforces this notion:

> Action springs out of what we fundamentally desire...the best advice for would-be persuaders, whether in business, the home, office, school, or politics is...first, arouse in the other person an eager want. He who can do this has the whole world with him. He who cannot walks a lonely way.

Manipulation, by contrast, is talking or acting without regard for other people's goals. It is distinctly different from the interpersonal dovetailing of influence.

The power of your communication is the result you get. If your communication is not getting you the results you want, then you need to alter your communication until you *do* see the outcome you want.

Earlier, we talked about using your instincts to discern manipulation. This ability to perceive motives, to understand the hidden desires of others, regardless of what is being said or done on the surface, is a vital influence skill.

People who develop this skill gain a great deal of self-understanding. They know what their goals are and become aware of their own strategies for fulfilling these goals. These skilled influencers learn to combine self-understanding with another important element, namely, self-confidence. These skills are the prerequisites of becoming an adept influencer.

The Technology of Influence

You've probably wondered what the "bits" are, the elements of behavior that lead to effective influence. Much research has been conducted in this area. The model presented in this book is based on work done by psychologists, sociologists, and organizational development experts. We have also conducted our own field studies on influence in the world of business. (The results of our latest study are described in the Appendix.)

What you'll find throughout this book is practical information about the "technology" of influence, the key elements that make up influence behavior.

The McBer group, a consulting company founded by David McClelland of Harvard, has been conducting research for many years to determine the specific skills—the "competencies," they call them—that make a person able to influence or persuade others. They have identified an array of skills and have some idea of how these skills develop. Often, skilled influencers begin sharpening their abilities during childhood. But one can learn influence skills at any time during life. After all, ability to influence is every bit as crucial for success in life as verbal agility or mathematical skill. It reflects a kind of intelligence that, until lately, has been slighted by the current emphasis on the more academic competencies.

Discovering Motives

Getting Tuned In

One of the most important influence skills, according to the latest research, is the ability to understand the true motives and desires of others *regardless of what is being said or done on the surface*. This finding supports our notion of trusting your uneasy feeling in communications with others, since these feelings often signal manipulation attempts. But the most skilled influencers are able to understand and empathize with others, whether the underlying motives of the others are positive or negative. Skilled influencers are simply tuned in.

Developing Self-Understanding

Skilled influencers also have a great deal of self-understanding. They know what their own goals are, they know what they are aiming for, and they are aware of their own strategies.

**Building Self-Confidence and a
Desire for Authority**

The Harvard researchers also found that skilled influencers com-
bined empathy and self-understanding with two other important
elements, namely, self-confidence and a desire for authority. The
result is a person who is able to reconcile his or her motives with
those of others in order to meet deadlines or to move toward a solution to problems that are either obvious and stated or subtle and unspoken.

Influencer Types

The researchers also defined three different types of influencers: the
directive, the collaborative, and the symbolic.

1. The *directive* type simply directs—or tells—people to do things in
   specific ways.
2. The *collaborative* type operates most effectively within groups. He or
   she uses social skills to gain cooperation and effect influence.
3. The *symbolic* type sets a personal example of how to be an achiever,
   and uses symbols to give a group an identity.

Influencing Patterns

Then there are the people who try to shortcut the influencing process.
These shortcuts fall into distinct patterns of behavior, so it's important
to watch out for them. You'll recognize these shortcuts because they create undue pressure. It isn't necessary to induce pressure if influence
skills are used effectively. Remember: Influence should be felt only in
its effect, not by exertion of force.

The Reciprocity Pattern

One shortcut pattern is reciprocity. Reciprocity occurs when we are influenced because we feel we owe a debt—either real or imagined—and we
want to repay it. There is an anecdote about Winston Churchill: After the
Prime Minister had a disagreement with someone, he gave them a nice
gift.

The Scarcity Pattern

Another pattern some influencers tend to use is scarcity, which communicates the feeling that something is in short supply. As a result, we may act too quickly and, unfortunately, make unwise decisions. Take, for example, the case of the portrait photographer who puts you on the defensive by giving you a special limited deal to sell you prints of photos he has taken of you. Your first impulse is to grab this "bargain" without realizing that *you* are in the power position. What is a photographer going to do with negatives of *your* picture? If you don't buy the pictures, there's no sale.

The point is, you often have a lot more power than you think.

So far, we've shown you that influence is an acquired skill, not an innate talent. We've also defined the general types of influence skills you will be learning.

While there are several different skills and modes of behavior essential to real influence, all of them have been incorporated into the *7 Secrets* approach. The result is a very simple model, which this book reveals, that you will find easy to apply to your professional and personal life.

In the next chapter you'll do some more exercises to help you establish your goals for learning influence skills. In subsequent chapters, you will take an influence skills inventory so you can identify what skills you're already using to influence people or situations, and you'll be introduced to a number of specific styles of influence and learn to recognize when people are using them.

2
Formulating Your Personal Influence Goals

As we've described various aspects of influence, you may have said to yourself, "Yes, I really need to sharpen up in that area..." or "I do that a lot. I have to learn how to stop doing that."

These are goals that you're setting for yourself. Before beginning any new enterprise, it's always a good idea to establish specific goals. The purpose of this chapter is to help you do that.

Influence Exercise 5: Creating a Personal Goal Sheet

In Exercise 5, you'll find a list of some of the goals that influence seminar participants have set for themselves. Comparing your influence goals to these may help you to bring your own personal goals for learning influence skills into sharper focus.

In the pages that follow, read each statement and check yes or no on line 1 to indicate whether each statement applies to your specific influence goals.

Once you've determined whether the statement represents a personal goal of yours, use question 2 to get a little more specific. In the space provided, write down the name of any individuals the statement brings to mind, such as your boss, a friend, or another person you'd like to influence.

To complete the third part, write down an action or actions you will take once you've learned the influence skills in this book.

Finally, in question 4, write down a positive outcome of fulfilling your goal.

As an example, let's work through the first one. First, is reading other people better something you want to accomplish? If so, check "yes" in the space provided. Now, write the name of the person or describe the particular situation you want to read more effectively. Next, write down an action you'll take to fulfill this goal once you've become more familiar with the skills of influencing, such as "I'll try to be more attentive to facial expressions when the person talks." Finally, write down a positive outcome of fulfilling this goal. For instance, "By being able to read Sophia (my boss) better, I'll be able to get more work done more efficiently." You may envision more than one positive outcome. The more, the better. Write down as many as you think are applicable.

Influence Exercise 5:
Personal Goals for *The 7 Secrets of Influence*

Learn to Read Other People and Situations Better

1. Yes_____   No_____

2. Who I want to influence: _____

3. What I can do to attain my goal: _____

_____

_____

_____

4. Positive outcome: _____

_____

_____

Learn Flexibility

1. Yes_____   No_____

2. Who I want to influence: _____

3. What I can do to attain my goal: _____

_____

_____

_____

4. Positive outcome: _____

_____

_____

Gain Cooperation from Previously Adversarial Individuals and Groups

1. Yes____   No____

2. Who I want to influence: _____

3. What I can do to attain my goal: _____

_____

_____

_____

4. Positive outcome: _____

_____

_____

Persuade Others to Support My Projects

1. Yes____   No____

2. Who I want to influence: _____

3. What I can do to attain my goal: _____

_____

_____

_____

4. Positive outcome: _____

_____

_____

(Continued)

Get More Information from People When It's Needed

1. Yes____   No____

2. Who I want to influence: _____

3. What I can do to attain my goal: _____

_____

_____

_____

4. Positive outcome: _____

_____

_____

Have More Credibility with Others

1. Yes____   No____

2. Who I want to influence: _____

3. What I can do to attain my goal: _____

_____

_____

_____

4. Positive outcome: _____

_____

_____

Sell My Ideas Inside as Well as Outside My Immediate Department or Group

1. Yes____   No ____

2. Who I want to influence: _____

3. What I can do to attain my goal: _____

_____

_____

_____

4. Positive outcome: _____

_____

_____

**Communicate Better within My Department
and with My Manager**

1. Yes____   No____

2. Who I want to influence: _____

3. What I can do to attain my goal: _____

_____

_____

_____

4. Positive outcome: _____

_____

_____

Listen and Respond Better to Others

1. Yes____   No____

2. Who I want to influence: _____

3. What I can do to attain my goal: _____

_____

_____

_____

4. Positive outcome: _____

_____

_____

Learn New Ideas and Apply These Ideas in My Communication

1. Yes____   No____

2. Who I want to influence: _____

(Continued)

3. What I can do to attain my goal: _____

_____

_____

_____

4. Positive outcome: _____

_____

_____

Communicate More Effectively with Others Outside My Immediate Group

1. Yes____   No____

2. Who I want to influence: _____

3. What I can do to attain my goal: _____

_____

_____

_____

4. Positive outcome: _____

_____

_____

Become More Effective at Meetings

1. Yes____   No____

2. Who I want to influence: _____

3. What I can do to attain my goal: _____

_____

_____

_____

4. Positive outcome: _____

_____

_____

Keep Meetings Moving Productively

1. Yes____   No____

2. Who I want to influence: _____

3. What I can do to attain my goal: _____

_____

_____

_____

4. Positive outcome: _____

_____

_____

Learn to Get More Information from People in My Organization

1. Yes____   No____

2. Who I want to influence: _____

3. What I can do to attain my goal: _____

_____

_____

_____

4. Positive outcome: _____

_____

_____

Become More Aware of and Open to the Different Styles of Those I Work With

1. Yes____   No____

2. Who I want to influence: _____

3. What I can do to attain my goal: _____

_____

_____

_____

(Continued)

4. Positive outcome: _____

_____

_____

Learn How to Create Cooperation

1. Yes____   No____

2. Who I want to influence: _____

3. What I can do to attain my goal: _____

_____

_____

_____

4. Positive outcome: _____

_____

_____

Identify and Expand My Base of Supporters

1. Yes____   No____

2. Who I want to influence: _____

3. What I can do to attain my goal: _____

_____

_____

_____

4. Positive outcome: _____

_____

_____

Get My Projects Supported by Upper Management

1. Yes____   No____

2. Who I want to influence: _____

3. What I can do to attain my goal: _____

_____

_____

_____

4. Positive outcome: _____

_____

Become Aware of More Options So I Don't Get Stuck

1. Yes____   No____

2. Who I want to influence: _____

3. What I can do to attain my goal: _____

_____

_____

_____

4. Positive outcome: _____

_____

_____

As a quick wrapup, here, in list form, are the model goals covered in Exercise 5:

- To learn to "read" other people and situations better.
- To learn flexibility.
- To get cooperation from previously adversarial individuals or groups.
- To persuade others to support my projects.
- To get more information from people when it's needed.
- To have more credibility with others.
- To sell my ideas inside as well as outside my immediate department or group.
- To communicate better within my department and with my manager.
- To listen and respond better to others.
- To learn new ideas and apply these ideas in my communication.

- To communicate more effectively with others outside my immediate group.
- To become more effective at meetings.
- To keep meetings moving productively.
- To learn to get more information from people in my organization.
- To become more aware of and open to the different styles of those I work with.
- To learn how to create cooperation.
- To identify and expand my base of supporters.
- To get my projects supported by upper management.
- To become aware of more options, so I don't get "stuck."

Influence Exercise 6:
Creating a Personal Influence
Action Plan

Now let's summarize from your Personal Goal Sheet. Do one or two names keep recurring? Is there a particular goal you want to achieve? Influence Exercise 6 will help you prepare an influence action plan for yourself—to help you focus more specifically on your goals. This exercise is designed to help you pinpoint a short-term, specific influence goal for that one person or situation that currently represents a challenge for you. Later, you may want to refer to this plan to change, refine, or update it.

First of all, who is the target of your influence strategy? Is it your boss? A peer? A subordinate? Or is it someone who has the power to stop your promotion or eliminate your pet project from the schedule? Write down the person's name and position in the space provided.

Second, what exactly do you want to change? Is it an action? Maybe it's inaction. Maybe you want this person to be more open with you. Or perhaps you would like to clear up a misunderstanding. Be clear and specific in the answer you give to question 2.

Third, what outcome do you envision if you succeed? Will you simply fulfill your immediate goal? Or will there be some long-term effect—either positive or negative? The implications of question 3 may require a little more thought.

Fourth, how will you know when you've gotten the result you want? What measurable, observable evidence will you need to ensure that your goal has been fulfilled? Is the person more friendly now? More open to

---

Influence Exercise 6: Influence Action Plan

1. *Who* do I want to influence? _____

_____

_____

_____

2. *What* behavior do I want to change in this person? _____

_____

_____

_____

_____

3. *What* will result if I manage to influence this change? _____

_____

_____

_____

_____

4. *How* will I know the result has been achieved?_____

_____

_____

_____

_____

5. *When* will I realistically influence this person and fulfill this goal?

_____

_____

---

your suggestions? Measuring results is critical to gauging success. You'd be surprised at how many people overlook this very important aspect of influencing.

Finally, when can you realistically expect to influence this person and fulfill your goal? Set a specific target date. It can be a year or six months from now — or even next week. But set a real date, write it in the space, and stick to it.

Save Exercise 6 so you can refer to it later. This constant reminder will help you achieve the goal you've set for yourself. You can also use this format as a model for setting future influence goals.

3
Influencing in an Age of Change

Every personal interaction is an influence interaction. The first two chapters showed you on a personal level how powerful and important a skill influencing can be. Now let's look at some of the signs that reinforce the notion that influencing is becoming a key skill in the current business environment.

Influence Scenario 1

Alienating People

Sandra, a technical specialist, supervised a small development group for a medical equipment manufacturer. She was well respected and well paid, but not considered to be on the so-called fast track. One day, while doing some research at a university hospital, she noticed an impressive piece of equipment that had been produced overseas.

Back in her office, Sandra kept thinking about the machine. After some tinkering on paper, she became convinced that her company could manufacture the unit better and less expensively than the foreign competitor.

Sandra then conducted some preliminary market research and found a large market for an improved version of the device. Armed with this data, she began to marshal interest in the project among her colleagues.

Soon, however, she started to run into small and subtle problems. Bills for the student she had hired as a research assistant were returned by the accounting department for further authorization.

The vice president of marketing abruptly canceled two meetings
with her and offered only thin excuses. Then her own boss,
although aware of her interest in the machine, assigned her to
another project and told her to put new-product development on
the back burner.

At first, Sandra thought she was just being paranoid. No one, she
told herself, was deliberately putting stumbling blocks in front of
her. Soon, however, she realized that even with the best of
intentions, her efforts had come to nothing. Despite her enthusiasm,
she had been unable to gain the support and cooperation she
needed from her colleagues, especially those in upper management.

What went wrong? Why wasn't Sandra able to get her project implemented? The reasons go beyond simple miscommunication. Sandra
failed to influence important people in her environment. For example,
instead of winning support for her project, Sandra may have unwit-
tingly alienated her colleagues by presenting them with finished plans,
rather than consulting them from the start.

Sandra's enthusiasm kept her from considering how to work most effectively in today's work environment. Her miscalculation led to a scenario repeated over and over again by otherwise successful managers.

In this chapter we will discuss why influence skills are needed today
more than ever, how the work environment affects influence and communication skills, and how to avoid the type of problems Sandra encountered.

Meeting the Challenge of an Age of Change

Whether you are a rookie in today's workplace or a seasoned veteran,
you'll be playing by a different set of rules. Behind these changes are
several new trends changing the way companies operate in the business
world. There are six areas in which big changes are happening:

Competition

Technology

Information

Worker values

Innovation

Organization

Below, you'll see exactly what the changes are, what's causing them, and how they affect your need for influence skills in the final decade of the century.

Competition—The Race Heats Up

In October 1987, the stock market crash brought an abrupt end to what has come to be known as the "expansive eighties." The frenzy of mergers and acquisitions ended, the hot specialty on Wall Street became bankruptcy law, and the country appeared to be on the verge of a recession.

Companies in Transition

For corporations and companies of all sizes, the emphasis has now changed to *streamlining, downsizing, cost containment,* and *belt-tightening,* either to guard against takeovers or to make the company more attractive to investors. The bottom line for employees: scarcer resources. You now face hotter and hotter competition with your colleagues for the basic resources, such as budgets, equipment, and support staff, that you need to do your job.

The Implications for Influence.   On a personal level, this trend means increased competition for project approvals, for choice assignments, for the attention of management, and for all the extras that you once may have taken for granted.

Competitiveness at Home and Abroad

Successfully competing within a company, however, won't mean anything unless your company itself is competitive. And today, influence that works is essential to maintaining competitiveness in national and world markets.

The Implications for Influence.   Influence skills are now a necessary part of the job, whether you're in marketing, public relations, sales, accounting, or purchasing. Knowing how to work well with people who control resources is to your advantage—and to your company's. Such skills are key to surviving in today's restrictive atmosphere.

Cultural Diversity

There's another dimension to this picture. Your suppliers, buyers, investors, and partners may be from a different culture. You may now be doing business with foreign-owned companies, foreign subsidiaries of your own company, or with the overseas headquarters of your own company. Soon, you may be doing business with a unified European marketplace and with developing countries jockeying for position in the global economy.

The Implications for Influence.   All this means increased global competition. You'll be competing with and for people who have different customs, cultural backgrounds, and communication habits. Finely tuned influence skills offer the only way to sure success in this new environment.

Technology—The Danger of Depersonalization

Our global economy is made possible by new communication technology, the second area of far-reaching change. These technologies, ranging from overnight delivery service and fax machines to integrated digital voice/data standards known as ISDN, are completely changing how business is conducted. Today we are connected as never before.

Wanted: One-on-One Skills for the New Team Environment

The gap between the technically knowledgeable and the technologically naive continues to widen. As a result, people who have technical jobs work more often on multifunction teams or task forces. More jobs require interdepartmental teams, or teams made up of people who do not typically work together and who may not even work at the same job site.

But as John Naisbitt, author of the best seller *Megatrends 2000*, points out, our high-tech capabilities have raced ahead of our "high-touch" needs. We are investing increasingly larger blocks of time and energy in learning how to use these new technologies most effectively. But as our communication becomes more technical, we are spending less time developing the interpersonal communication skills that enable us to produce the best product or provide the best service that we can.

You can't get agreement or support for what you want without communicating your desires clearly.

Information—Getting What You Need

Try to imagine the marketplace 40 years ago. No copy machines, no overnight mail, and no modems to connect you with, say, a supplier or client. Managers had much less information to work with. Today's increase in technology has prompted a parallel increase in information. Information now comes to us in mind-boggling quantities and at split-second speeds. And as we rapidly move from an industrial economy based on manufacturing to a service economy, the flow of information only quickens.

Influencing Information Flow

Yet the problem is not the overflow of information but the distribution of this information throughout an organization. Getting information to the right person at the right time can mean the success or failure of major deals. And it can save enormous amounts of money that would otherwise be spent duplicating efforts. Getting all the information you need also presents new challenges.

The Implications for Influence.   It's like putting together a jigsaw puzzle. There are people who have some pieces of it. But in order to complete the puzzle—to get the whole picture—the rest of the pieces must be acquired from other people. The secret of success is being able to gain the cooperation of all the right people. And that's where influence comes in.

New Worker Values Require New Management Norms

In the not-too-distant past, individuals worked quite autonomously. We rarely knew what the next person up the ladder did in our own company—much less what people did in other companies. Information on how we do our jobs has now become more accessible. We're not as secretive as we once were. There is less physical space and less job differentiation between us and the people below and above us.

As a result, employees are developing different job expectations. This represents a radical change in worker values.

Influence Scenario 2

Trading Taskmasters for Facilitators

Tim, for example, was a "tough guy" manager, unsympathetic, distant, and secretive. He not only ordered his subordinates — he threatened them. But the bottom line was low morale, low productivity, and high turnover. Tim's employees took whatever opportunities they found to transfer to other departments. Finally Tim turned to a management training seminar. Eventually he realized that his job was not to boss his people but to provide leadership to help them figure out how to get their jobs done best.

These days Tim exerts much less control but has a much more productive, stable staff.

The Implications for Influence. Employees no longer tolerate bossy managers who act like dictators or commanding officers. Instead of simply following arbitrary orders, workers want to take part actively in decision making. This new expectation has created a need for a different type of manager.

As Tim learned, the most successful managers today are more open and encourage participation and two-way communication. Managers who remain closed or secretive risk alienating people both above and below them in the corporate structure. Corporations now look for managers with the right people skills.

Innovation—We're All Expected to Be More Creative

The new work force of more responsive and responsible workers and more open managers has increased the demand for internal innovation. More and more companies are demanding increased creativity from their workers in return for increased career control.

Companies are looking for innovative ideas concerning internal structure as well as external competition. Workers and managers are asked to become "intrapreneurs"—innovators who work inside a corporate structure to create smaller business units, which operate almost independently of the parent organization.

No longer is creativity the exclusive province of the marketing or advertising departments. In today's most successful companies, all areas—

manufacturing, management information systems, accounting, human resources, and research and development—are hotbeds of innovation and creativity.

The Implications for Influence. Successfully implementing these new ideas and creative solutions calls for highly developed communication and influence skills. The innovator needs the ability to sell an idea to the decision makers. We've all seen a great idea die a premature death or gather dust in a file drawer because its creator lacked influence skills. One such example is Sandra, mentioned at the beginning of this chapter.

Organizational Structure— Changing the Way Things Work

The five trends discussed so far have contributed to a sixth change, namely, reorganization. Corporations are now undergoing their most sweeping structural changes since Alfred Sloan instituted decentralized management at General Motors in the 1920s. These changes cut across industry lines, geography, and corporate size.

Top-Down Is Out

Most companies have been formally structured from the top down on a strict military or hierarchical model, as shown in Figure 3-1. Upper management sits at the top of a pyramid, with varying layers of middle managers in the middle, and hundreds of supervisors and workers below. Orders issued at the top filter down through the organization. A single group of top individuals makes decisions; influence is top-down.

Flatter and Less Formal Is In

Today, however, the way companies work is becoming less formal and relationships throughout a typical organization are starting to change.

Companies are taking decentralization to its logical conclusion, and the corporate structure itself is changing, as you can see in Figure 3-2. The layers of middle management—the corporate overseers—are being reduced in some companies by, estimates say, as much as 80 percent. In one study of top corporations, those with the best performance records had fewer than four management layers, and those with the worst had as many as eight.

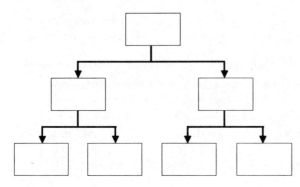

Characterized by:

- Subordinate-boss relationships
- Decisions made at top, executed below
- Management skills: Leadership, planning, controlling, organizing, and integrating people and resources for efficient and effective work production, coaching, counseling, goal and task definition, performance appraisal

Problems solved by:

- Authority
- Procedure
- Management decision

Decisions are:

- Made by single person or with the consensus of a small group of specialists
- Implemented by direction

Relationships are:

- Defined by structure based on loyalty, obedience, leadership

Figure 3-1. Hierarchical organizational structure.

The Implications for Influence.   In this new organizational structure, the way things get done, especially by people in the middle and by staff or "individual contributors," is through influence.

Coercion or formal authority, useful in the old model, no longer works. The influence must be subtle and sincere to get decisions made *upward* with managers, *downward* with subordinates, and *laterally* with peers and coworkers.

Shifts in corporate structures mean we have to work with others without benefit of a clear reporting relationship Thus we have to influence people over whom we have no formal authority. The way you communicate changes when decisions require support and participation from others who have the resources, skills, and information you need.

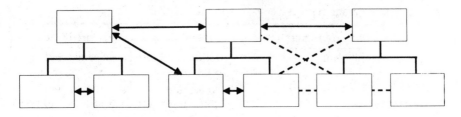

Characterized by:
- Peer, no-authority relationships
- Decisions made by collaboration and involvement
- Management skills: Linking people by being supportive, helpful; sharing power; building trust to serve mutual interests; sharing resources, advice, and aid; performing work efficiently and effectively

Problems solved by:
- Using support and help to establish ground rules for efficiently handling issues

Decisions are:
- Made by sharing power so that alternatives are offered from diverse perspectives and systematically evaluated
- Made by collaboration

Relationships are:
- Based on mutual trust

Figure 3-2. Flat organizational structure.

Caught in the Middle

If you're in the middle of an organization you're caught between those above you, whom you are supposed to *serve*, and those below you, whom you must *manage*. In both cases, you must use influence to get the results you want, even though you may not have the organizationally sanctioned power or authority to do so.

So, as a manager or worker, the demands on you are considerable:

- You have to work through others with whom there are often no clear reporting relationships.
- You often have more responsibility than authority.
- There may be no clearly defined goals or criteria for your success.

This is summarized in Table 3-1.

Table 3-1. Management Skills versus Influence Skills

Management skills are required when:	Influence skills are required when:
Decisions are unilateral.	Decisions require participation and support.
You are in control over people, resources, projects.	Others have expertise, information, contacts, or resources you need to get results.
Issues are simple, predictable, linear.	Issues are complex, unpredictable, nonlinear.
Impact is on single units or departments.	Impact is on multiple units ("ripple effect").
Impact and concerns are narrow, contained.	Organizational impact and concerns are broad.
Results are obtained by controlling, directing, and evaluating.	Results are obtained by spontaneity and responsiveness to organizational needs.
Structures are preset.	Structures emerge from assessing issues and setting goals.
You have official recognition.	You need informal support.
You have extrinsic power.	You need intrinsic power.
You work with autonomy.	Success is achieved through interdependence.
The "territory" is defined and contained.	There is territorial overlap.
You are directing.	You are negotiating, persuading.

Playing It by Ear

Even though the conditions necessitating good influence skills are likely to emerge in today's business world, in which major structural change is rapidly taking place, you shouldn't eliminate the old management skills from your repertoire. There are clearly certain circumstances that require influence and others that require traditional management. To know when influence is called for, refer to Table 3-1. For example, when your area of control or authority is clear cut, basic managerial skills are needed.

However, methods must change when decisions require support and participation from others who are outside your sphere of authority; the right method is determined by the situation itself.

Think back to the example of Sandra, who was introduced at the beginning of this chapter. She didn't understand how to gain support from those outside her sphere of influence. She didn't check what was competing with her for management attention. Neither did she collaborate and gain her colleagues' cooperation and participation before launching into her presentations.

She didn't realize that the data she hired a market researcher to gather was already available in the company in another department. All she needed to do was to communicate her intentions and make a contact.

Without support from her staff or other people in the department, her boss didn't give her idea much credence. The vice president of marketing didn't want to go over the head of Sandra's boss, and so he wouldn't meet with her.

So, what may have been a great idea was squashed before it had a chance simply because Sandra didn't pay attention to all the influence work that needed to be done. She was playing by an old set of rules. She failed because she was not sensitive — tuned in — to the organizational and human realities of her situation.

Getting Ahead in the Age of Change

The environmental changes discussed in this chapter are bringing about another set of radical changes. These are the changes in the way we deal with our careers.

It's Not What You Know

It used to be that when we started up the corporate ladder, we were told that in order to achieve success we simply needed to put in our time and to develop our professional and technical expertise.

It's Not Who You Know

After a while, this began to change and we heard that "it's not what you know, it's who you know." We began to learn the importance of contacts, and how to build a network of helpful people.

So What Is It?

Now we have entered a new era. You can't count on technical or professional expertise alone. These skills can quickly become obsolete. And you can't simply count on your contacts to get what you want. High-level contacts can vanish overnight with the next corporate shake-up, budget cut, acquisition, or merger. What you need is something of your own, an inner resource or ability which you can tap whenever it's called for. What you need, in short, is *influence*: a set of people skills that can serve you whenever and wherever you are, a set of interpersonal skills that you can practice anytime, anywhere, inside or outside an organization. We call it "portable power."

Mastery of influence skills represents a strategic approach to moving ahead in today's world. As we've said, influence is not an inherent gift or talent, but a set of skills that anyone can learn, practice, and master.

Influence Exercise 7: Your Own Organization

As you go through this book and learn new concepts of influence, think about the people you work with and their relationship to you. You'll want to apply the skills we discuss directly to these relationships since they are of the most immediate importance to you. Exercise 7 will help you think about these issues.

Influence Exercise 7: Your Company's Structure

For this exercise, draw a diagram of *your* organization. Make sure to put yourself in the chart. Then, answer the following four questions.

My Organization

---

1. What are the underlying forces that have created this structure? Think about the trends in the new work environment. Which of these has had the greatest effect on your company, and why?

_____

_____

_____

_____

2. Write down the names of three people in the boxes that are connected to yours by whatever lines you drew. Next, ask yourself what are the major differences between you and the people in the adjoining boxes? Do they have more or different skills? More or less power? Write these differences next to each name you wrote. _____

_____

_____

_____

_____

_____

3. What do you have in common with these people? Do they have the same skills? Are you on the same level? _____

_____

_____

_____

_____

4. Is each of these people resistant to you or receptive to you? If they are resistant to you, state why. Are there power differences? A personality clash?

_____

_____

_____

_____

Influence Exercise 8:
Trends in Today's Workplace

Now let's examine the changes discussed at the beginning of this chapter. How many of these changes or trends are taking place in your company? Are they having an impact on you? If so, how? Write your answers in the work space provided in Exercise 8.

Influence Exercise 8: Trends in Today's Workplace

COMPETITION

Has your company recently merged with another company or bought another company, creating overlapping positions? How has your company's competitive position changed?

How have you been affected by these changes? How have your company's competitive changes affected you?

How your company is affected: _____

_____

_____

_____

_____

_____

_____

_____

How you are affected: _____

_____

_____

_____

_____

_____

_____

TECHNOLOGY

How in the past few years has your company increased the amount of technology it uses? How has this increased technology affected the way your company works, both internally and externally? Write down two examples.

How has this technology affected you? Have you been able to keep up with it?

How your company is affected: _____

_____

_____

_____

_____

_____

_____

_____

_____

_____

How you are affected: _____

_____

_____

_____

_____

_____

_____

_____

_____

_____

(Continued)

INFORMATION

How has your company been making or demanding more information?
How has increased information been handled by your company?

How has this increased information affected you recently?
How your company is affected: _____

_____

_____

_____

_____

_____

_____

_____

_____

_____

_____

How you are affected: _____

_____

_____

_____

_____

_____

_____

_____

_____

_____

_____

_____

WORKER VALUES

Has upper management recently been soliciting employee input on long- or short-term goals? Have managers within your group or department been doing the same? How have changing worker values — new expectations — affected your company?

Have you as an employee recently asked for an increased role in your group? Or, have you as a manager recently allowed more input from your staff? How have changing worker values affected you?

How your company is affected: _____

_____

_____

_____

_____

_____

_____

_____

_____

_____

How you are affected: _____

_____

_____

_____

_____

_____

_____

_____

(Continued)

INNOVATION

Has your company spun off any "intrapreneurial" groups? Or, has upper management started asking its groups for more innovative thinking? How has your company been affected by innovation?

How have you become more innovative recently?

How your company is affected: _____

_____

_____

_____

_____

_____

_____

_____

_____

_____

_____

How you are affected: _____

_____

_____

_____

_____

_____

_____

_____

_____

_____

_____

_____

_____

_____

ORGANIZATIONAL STRUCTURE

Has upper management restructured recently? Or have they asked for more interdivisional cooperation? How has your company's performance been changed by structural changes?

Have you been asked to sit in on meetings of other groups recently? Or, have you had to seek input from a completely different division in order to complete a project? How has corporate restructuring affected you?

How your company is affected: _____

_____

_____

_____

_____

_____

_____

_____

How you are affected: _____

_____

_____

_____

_____

_____

_____

_____

Once you've finished making these notes, you're likely to see that workplace changes are having a larger effect on you than you may have thought. The changes you are encountering require that you be more influential in your dealings with new and different people and an organizational structure. In the next chapters, you'll learn how.

4

Discovering Your Personal Influence Style

Now, let's examine how you currently speak when you're trying to influence someone.

Influence Exercise 9: Profiling Your Current Modus Operandi

How do you influence people? Do you stop, listen, and watch yourself as you try to sway someone's opinion or change someone's behavior? If you're like most people, you probably don't really know how you influence others.

As mentioned in Chapter 1, understanding your own "technology" of influence is the beginning of mastering influence skills in all situations. The questions in Exercise 9 are designed to help you become aware of how you usually behave when you're trying to influence.

Influence Exercise 9: Preliminary Modus Operandi Self-Profile

1. How you have influenced someone:

   A. Describe a recent situation in which you influenced someone to believe or do something different.

   _____

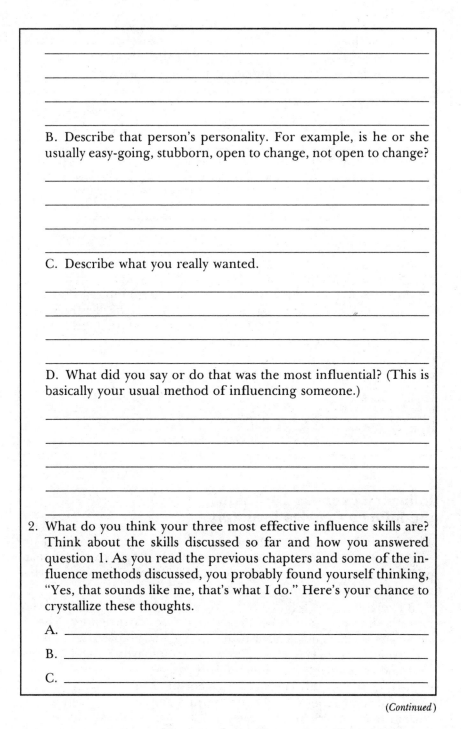

B. Describe that person's personality. For example, is he or she usually easy-going, stubborn, open to change, not open to change?

C. Describe what you really wanted.

D. What did you say or do that was the most influential? (This is basically your usual method of influencing someone.)

2. What do you think your three most effective influence skills are? Think about the skills discussed so far and how you answered question 1. As you read the previous chapters and some of the influence methods discussed, you probably found yourself thinking, "Yes, that sounds like me, that's what I do." Here's your chance to crystallize these thoughts.

A. _____

B. _____

C. _____

(Continued)

3. What influence skills would you like to improve? Again, you may, as you've read, have said to yourself, "I wish I could do that better," when a particular influence method was discussed.

A. _____

B. _____

C. _____

4. Who do you need to influence to further your career? Try to stick with names this time, not titles, since influencing someone is easier if you know them. Try to limit the number of names to three.

A. _____

B. _____

C. _____

5. Describe a current situation and an individual, not a group, you'd like to influence. What do you want this person to do, think, or change? For example, maybe you'd like that higher-level job just vacated by a coworker. Or maybe you'd like to turn a difficult client around to your way of thinking.

_____

_____

_____

_____

Influence Exercise 10: Taking the Influence Styles Inventory

To begin improving your influencing powers, you must begin by understanding your personal influence style. Each of us has a different approach that we use to get the results we want. Some are more effective than others.

In Exercise 10 you'll find a sampling of 12 questions from a psychological testing program called the Influence Styles Inventory. The inventory is a self-assessment instrument that was prepared by training professionals, management experts, and psychologists. While a complete and accurate interpretation of your style should be done only by a trained instructor, this inventory segment will help you pinpoint what specific style or styles of influence you use and how to recognize and react to similar styles in other people.

Influence Exercise 10: The Influence Styles Inventory

Read each pair of statements and decide which statement most accurately describes you when you are attempting to influence someone. Even if you feel that neither statement fits you perfectly, choose the one that most closely applies to your behavior or attitude. Indicate your choice with a check mark on the line to the right of the statement.

Example: In the pair below, if you feel that the statement, "When someone presents a 'blue sky' idea, I bring them back to reality" describes you better than "I present my ideas by appealing to emotions, not logic," then you would check line *a* as shown below:

a. When someone presents a 'blue sky' idea, I bring
them back to reality   *a.* ____
b. I present my ideas by appealing to emotions, not logic   *b.* ____

A few guidelines:

1. Work quickly and intuitively. Chances are the first answer you choose for each question is the right one for you.
2. Don't try to base your answer on what you think is socially desirable. There is no right or wrong way. Just respond in the way that's most true for you.
3. Don't worry about apparent inconsistencies. You'll notice that some of the phrases come up more than once. You may be tempted to answer the same way you did in the previous occurrence, but keep in mind that the repeated statement is being paired with a different statement. Just answer each item as a totally discrete and separate question.
4. For now, disregard the numbers to the right of each answer line.
5. It may be helpful for you to have a particular influence situation in mind as you go through these questions. Or you may want to focus on your usual modus operandi—the way you normally behave when trying to influence someone.

1. *a.* When someone presents a "blue sky" idea, I bring
   them back to reality.   *a.* ____3
   b. I present my ideas by appealing to emotions,
   not logic.   *b.* ____6

2. *a.* I always tell people specifically how my ideas
   benefit them.   *a.* ____5
   b. I believe in telling people what you need from
   them and what you're willing to give in return.   *b.* ____2

(Continued)

3. *a.* If someone disagrees, I respond by offering
      solid evidence.   *a.* ____1
   b. I often change my ideas after hearing the
      opinions of others.   *b.* ____4

4. *a.* I get others to act by establishing a shared mission. *a.* ____6
   b. I let people know up front what I expect of them. *b.* ____2

5. *a.* I'm satisfied when people agree to only a piece of
      what I'm proposing.   *a.* ____5
   b. I offer detailed logical plans about a job that needs
      to be done.   *b.* ____1

6. *a.* My communication style can change considerably,
      depending on whom I'm talking to.   *a.* ____4
   b. I can quickly zero in on people's mistaken
      assumptions.   *b.* ____3

7. *a.* When possible, I use the authority of higher
      management to help get my ideas accepted.   *a.* ____2
   b. I try to discover what motivates each person when
      I'm trying to influence others.   *b.* ____5

8. *a.* I'll readily admit my lack of expertise when I'm
      trying to influence others.   *a.* ____4
   b. In selling my ideas, I use images and metaphors
      of a better future.   *b.* ____6

9. *a.* I'll challenge an idea that won't work.   *a.* ____3
   b. When I'm trying to influence people, I appeal to
      their dreams and ideals.   *b.* ____6

10. *a.* I recognize that reward is a strong motivator. *a.* ____2
    b. When trying to influence others, I take the time
       to figure out people's individual decision making
       styles.   *b.* ____5

11. *a.* When presenting my ideas, I actively encourage
       the suggestions and ideas of others.   *a.* ____4
    b. Reason and logic are effective tools in influencing
       others.   *b.* ____1

12. *a.* I'll point out flaws, mistakes, or inconsistencies
       in the proposals or ideas of others.   *a.* ____3
    b. I present my ideas by appealing to logic,
       rather than emotion.   *b.* ____1

There are, as will be explained in Part 2, six different basic styles of influence. Your current style will fall into one of these six categories; that is, one of the six styles will distinguish the way you now go about trying to get the results you want. It's your preferred influence style. By introducing you to these styles and showing you how to use them to your advantage, you will be learning, in essence, the first six secrets of influence. To benefit from the seventh and final secret, which you will learn in Part 3, you must first learn all six basic styles on which successful influence is based.

Once you've completed the Influence Styles Inventory, you should tally your answers. Tallying involves the numbers 1 through 6 at the end of each answer line. Each number corresponds to one of six distinct influence styles that will be explained in detail later on.

Figure 4-1 shows your Influence Styles Inventory score sheet. Across the top of the score sheet are the numbers 1 through 6. Go through your inventory. If you answered *a* for question 1, you'll see a 3 to the right of your check mark. So place a slash mark on the score sheet in column 3, as shown in the example in Figure 4-2. If your answer to question 1 was *b*, place a slash in column 6 of your score sheet. If you answered *a* on question 2, place a slash in column 5 of your score sheet, and so on with the remainder of the 12 questions.

Now, add all the slashes in column 1 and put the total in the totals row at the bottom. Do the same for column 2, and so on for the six columns.

Influence Styles Inventory Score Sheet						
T	C	F	W	S	G	
1	2	3	4	5	6	
Totals						= 12

Figure 4-1. Influence Styles Inventory score sheet.

Influence Styles Inventory Score Sheet						
T	C	F	W	S	G	
1	2	3	4	5	6	
I	III	II	I	II	III	
Totals	1	3	2	1	2	3	= 12

Figure 4-2. Sample of filled-in Influence Styles Inventory score sheet.

Now add your totals across to make sure they add up to 12. If they don't, you missed a question somewhere. Find out which one or ones and make the proper corrections.

Each column represents a different influence style, as you may have guessed. The column with the highest total is the style you use most frequently. Before moving on to an interpretation of your inventory results, there is one more essential exercise I'd like you to complete.

Influence Exercise 11:
The Fitness Center

The purpose of Exercise 11 is to move beyond theory and give you an opportunity to practice influencing a number of people to get a project off the ground.

Imagine that you're a member of a team or task force that is in charge of designing and building a new fitness center for your company's employees. The goal is to plan a strategy for communicating the concept of this center throughout your company, from line employees to upper management.

Make your strategy plan as if you were trying to set up this fitness center in your own company. Write down the names and titles of people with whom you would speak, what kind of research you would need to do, what department heads you think must be involved, and how you would get their input. Try to be as precise as possible, and include how you would communicate your ideas. For instance, would you send a memo? Call organized meetings? Meet informally? What information would you need? Where would you get this information? Write down a couple of key phrases that you would use.

The objective is not to find out how much you know about putting together a fitness center. What's more important is to see how you'd go about putting together a plan, how you'd communicate your ideas to other people, and how you'd use influence to achieve your objective. In Part 2, as part of the discussion of each of the six basic styles of influence, you will be shown how other people planned a fitness center. By comparing your plan with theirs, not only will you discover more about your own style, you will discover the wide range of other possible styles which you can master.

Since everyone has their own way of deciding what strategy to follow in Exercise 11, you will not be given any clues on how to proceed except for the headings. These should be used as guidelines only. It's up to you to decide which factors are most important and in what sequence your strategies should be presented.

Influence Exercise 11: The Fitness Center

The Center: _____

_____

_____

_____

_____

_____

Equipment: _____

_____

_____

_____

_____

Budget: _____

_____

_____

_____

_____

Physical design: _____

_____

_____

_____

_____

Services: _____

_____

_____

_____

_____

Users: _____

_____

(*Continued*)

```
  _____
  _____
  _____

  Communicated to: _____

  _____
  _____
  _____
  _____

  Via: _____

  _____
  _____
  _____
  _____
```

After you've completed Exercise 11, review your plan. How thorough were you in your approach? Did you hit all the necessary levels of management? Did you note what methods you would use to communicate your ideas?

Look over your plan one more time. If you think you missed anything, now is the time to finish filling in the blanks. When you're satisfied, you can move on to Part 2. There, in addition to finding out your preferred influence style, you will be given descriptions of all the styles and the opportunity to compare your fitness center plan with those of people whose influence styles are different from yours.

PART 2

The First Six Secrets Revealed

When you prepared your plan for the fitness center, did you use facts and logic? Did you decide to talk to a variety of people before finalizing your plan? Did you try to get people excited about the project, appealing to their emotions, in order to set up your presentation? Did you simply use your position of authority to get your plans approved?

Each of these methods represents a different style of influence. Here in Part 2, you'll find out the results of your Influence Styles Inventory. I'll describe each of the six styles of influence and how you can recognize and deal with these styles in other people.

It is important to keep in mind that each influence style is a set of behaviors, not merely a type of person, though the behavior of some people may conform to a certain style to a degree that invites stereotyping. When learning each of the basic styles, you will find it helpful to think of someone you know who represents that style. However, since you would use a particular style to suit a particular situation, try to think of the styles as strategies of influencing rather than personality traits.

In identifying each style, I've taken some poetic license. I've given each one a convenient label to make it easier to remember. All the names rhyme so that they will resonate a little more, and therefore be a little more memorable.

The six styles, listed in the sequence from your score sheet, are:

1. Telling, or the Analyst
2. Compelling, or the Pragmatist
3. Felling, or the Preservationist
4. Welling, or the Catalyst
5. Selling, or the Strategist
6. Gelling, or the Idealist

No one is truly and definitively just a Teller or a Geller. What I'm calling "styles" are actually clusters of behaviors or attitudes. Another thing to remember is that the numbering sequence does not indicate hierarchy. No single style is *better* or *worse* than another. Each is useful and effective in certain situations or with certain people, and each has its benefits as well as its limitations.

Now look back at your score sheet for the Influence Styles Inventory. The category you got the highest score in is the style—or influence strategy—that you use most often, and the one that comes most naturally to you. In the chapters that follow we'll examine each style so you can begin to understand how you already use a combination of them.

5
Secret #1:
The Telling/Analyst Style

If you scored highest in the first column of the Influence Styles Inventory score sheet in Chapter 4, Telling is your predominant style. Telling is the influence style characterized by the use of logic, facts, opinions, and ideas. As an example of people who use the Telling style, think of Sherlock Holmes or *Star Trek*'s Mr. Spock as extreme Tellers.

Doing It Head to Head

People who use the Telling style are direct in presenting their ideas, which they support with evidence and arguments. This style relies on logic, reason, and factual evidence as a method of persuading, rather than on appeals to emotion. Often, lawyers use this style in their cool courtroom presentations of facts and evidence. People who use the Telling style are generally good with words and quick to defend their ideas with logical argument. They have analytical minds. They value structure and organization. When they integrate their ideas with those of others, they usually do so by fitting them into the logical structure of what has already been established. They are usually keenly aware of the organization and order of things, and they like to follow policies and procedures. In short, Telling is the style of the *analyst*.

Where's the Beef?

Although it can be a powerful style, Telling may not always work because humans are not influenced solely by reason or valid ideas. It is often difficult to change feelings with facts. The Telling style is similar to the "Directive" style described by the management experts at Harvard.

The Telling style can be most effective when:

- You already have, or are sure you can build, credibility with the person(s) you are trying to influence.

- You are the only readily available authority or source of information on the topic under discussion.

- Other independent authorities or sources of information support your position on the matter.

- The person(s) you are trying to influence perceive that their own interests and goals are shared by you; they see you as "on the same side" or as "one of us."

- You want to influence someone whose mode or style of communication is, like yours, one of logic, facts, and reason, and who makes decisions based on the evidence and the logical weighing of pros and cons.

The Telling style can be ineffective when creative solutions or new ideas are needed or when you're exploring uncharted areas.

To influence Tellers, you must speak their language. Because they are so fact-oriented, they might like some numbers and statistics to back up what you propose. They'd certainly appreciate a rational discussion of the issues, and they care a lot about substance. "Where's the beef?" would be a question asked by a Teller, if he feels he's just been getting "fluff" or a peripheral discussion. Not only do Tellers want as many hard facts as you have, but they want them presented in a logical, structured way. And at the beginning of a presentation, they want to know what the procedures and ground rules are. They don't like surprises or things that come out of the blue.

Listening for "Telling" Words

Some of the inventory statements that describe the Telling style are:

- I try to present my ideas by appealing to logic, not emotion.
- I offer detailed, logical plans about a job that needs to be done.

- If someone disagrees, I respond by offering solid evidence.
- Reason and logic are extremely effective tools in influencing others.
- Here are some clues to give you an idea of whether someone is using the Telling style. Sometimes a word or two isn't enough to really give you an accurate picture, but you may sense a pattern if a person repeatedly uses the kinds of words or phrases associated with Telling. You will begin to notice them as you listen for them in people's conversations. Tellers tend to say things like:

"Let me *tell* you…"

"Let me *show* you…"

"The *rationale* for this project is…"

"The *facts* state…"

"The *data demonstrate*…"

Other words to look for are *explain, reasons, evidence, structure,* and *organize.*

Telling in Action

In actual seminars, we placed people in groups based on how they scored on the inventory. For instance, all the people who scored highest in category 1 were grouped together. We grouped all the number 2s, all the number 3s, and so on. Then each group was given about 15 minutes to come up with a strategy for getting acceptance from upper management for an in-house corporate fitness center. At the end of the time allotted, each group had someone make a mock presentation to upper management. We've simulated six condensed versions of these reports. Here's the first one, from the Telling group. The words and phrases in **bold italic** type are those that distinguish the Telling style from the other influence styles.

The Fitness Center
The Telling Point of View

*Well, we wanted to put together all the specifics of the fitness center so we could tell the employees what would be in it and to let upper management know what it was all going to cost. So we put together this **outline** to enable us to approach the problem in a **structured, step-by-step way**.*

*__First__ of all, we had to figure out how much room there was, and where the center was going to be. We thought the center should be in the main corporate building, **so people wouldn't have to travel**—and we wanted it to be easy to* *get to, so people would use it more frequently. Since it was in our building this put a limit on our space. In view of the **fact** that we were making this up, we **calculated** we had 2,500 square feet.*

*Second, once we knew how much square footage we had, we **made a list** of the equipment and facilities the center would have. We thought we should have Nautilus and free weights rather than racquetball or other recreational or competitive facilities, **because** we thought it would be easier to get insurance if there wasn't any competition sport between people.*

*Third, we tried to **figure out** how much everything was going to cost. We figured x number of dollars for the equipment. Then, we had to add in a locker room, showers, and supplies like towels and locks and so forth, and at least two people to run the center. To sell the idea to upper management, we thought it would be best to come up with a monthly cost—a dollar figure—that we could **compare** it with the potential savings in health insurance, increased productivity, and less sick time.*

*Once we knew what the center was going to be, we had to start **telling** people. We sent a memo to the facilities' director to let him know what we were doing, and we asked him to start getting **cost quotes** for design and construction. Once we had these **figures**, we felt we could make a presentation to upper management. Once upper management approved, we would send out a memo to employees to **inform** them of what we had come up with in terms of how it would benefit them and the company as a whole.*

Did your report sound anything like this? Did you formulate everything you thought should be in the center and simply tell people what was happening? Try to compare your approaches to the problem with the strategies in this and the other simulated reports in the chapters that follow.

Influence Exercise 12: The Telling Style

By now, you should have a good idea of what the Telling style of influence is all about. By completing Exercise 12, you can test your understanding of this style and then identify one or more people you know who are typical Tellers. Here's a summary of the characteristics of the Telling style. A Teller/Analyst:

- Prefers logic over emotion.
- Justifies arguments or ideas with reasons and evidence.
- Values structure and organization.
- Likes to integrate and link into others' points.
- Is inclined to elaborate on positions.

Influence Exercise 12: The Telling Style

Now see how many of the characteristics of the Telling style you can recall. Then use the rest of this exercise to record your understanding of Telling, in yourself and in others.

Characteristics of the style:

1. _____

2. _____

3. _____

4. _____

5. _____

Person(s) I know who use this style:

1. _____

2. _____

3. _____

4. _____

Examples of their behavior (or how I know they're Tellers):

1. _____

2. _____

3. _____

4. _____

Strengths of the Telling style:

1. _____

2. _____

3. _____

4. _____

Weaknesses of the Telling style:

1. _____

2. _____

3. _____

4. _____

6
Secret #2: The Compelling/ Pragmatist Style

If you scored high in the second category of the inventory in Chapter 4, then you primarily use the Compelling style. Compelling is the style of the pragmatist. This style of influence is used when one has legitimate · authority in a situation—typically in a boss-subordinate relationship.

Doing It with Authority

When you have more power than another person, you can make demands, set standards, and rely on that person's acceptance of a subordinate role—in addition to an underlying fear or insecurity—to make sure that you get what you want. As an example of a Compeller, think of a school teacher or a sports coach.

Compelling may take the form of offering rewards for compliance or threatening punishment or deprivation for noncompliance. It may involve the use of organizational power, or more indirectly, veiled pressures may be exerted through the use of status, prestige, or formal authority, as well as by outlining the trade-offs in a situation.

People who use this style let others know up front what they want, expect, or require of them, and what standards will be used in judging performance. They then follow up to find out what has been done, administering approval or disapproval, praise or blame, and rewards or punishments (or withholding of privileges), as they are called for. The rewards and punishments may be psychological (approval, acceptance, rejection, respect) as well as economic or material.

When You Have the Upper Hand

The Compelling style is most effective when the other person's level of motivation or need for the rewards you control is high. A disadvantage of this style, however, is that the influence attempt may be successful only as long as the motivators—rewards and punishments—keep coming. When they are removed, the behavior or concessions they motivate tend to slacken or even stop. When deeper and lasting changes in behavior are desired or stronger commitment is required, other influence styles are more effective.

Using the Compelling style only with rewards and incentives, avoiding bossy pressures and punishments, creates much less resistance to the influence attempt. This version of the style ignores undesired behavior and rewards desired behavior (with praise, for example). Its disadvantage is that most people find it very difficult to ignore annoying or substandard behavior on the part of others. Not only that, but people who use the Compelling form of influence tend to smooth over differences too quickly. The "nice guy" Compeller who avoids unpleasant yet necessary confrontations may ultimately fail, like the parent who spoils by sparing the rod. Once the other person is spoiled, it's hard for the Compeller to turn things around. Unlike the Weller (whose style is discussed in Chapter 8), the Compeller does not use listening and self-disclosure skills to establish good working relationships.

The Compelling style is similar to the techniques described in *The One Minute Manager*; that is, offering praise and criticism and rewards and punishments when they're appropriate. People who use this style are practical—which is why we also call them "pragmatists"—and extremely results-oriented. They want to see their ideas happen. They want to hear "Mission accomplished." Furthermore, they believe in the old saying: When all else fails, follow directions.

Listening for "Compelling" Words

If you scored high as a Compeller, some of the inventory statements that you checked included:

- I recognize that reward is a strong motivator.
- When possible, I use the authority of higher management to help get my ideas accepted.
- I let people know up front what is required of them.
- I believe in telling people what I need from them and what I'm willing to give in return.

It is helpful to recognize the kinds of expressions Compellers use in a situation that calls for influence. They frequently involve some kind of trade-off, such as:

"I'll do *x* if you'll do *y*."

"*Upper management fully supports* this effort."

"We *expect to achieve...*"

"The *positive rewards* from this include..."

Such expressions reveal the structured, down-to-earth, results-oriented focus of this influence style.

Compelling in Action

Here's the account of how a planning group attempts to use the Compelling style—rather than Telling, as demonstrated in the previous chapter—to establish an in-house fitness center. **Boldface italic** words and phrases are typical of Compellers.

The Fitness Center
The Compelling Point of View

*We thought the most important thing was to set up a series of **short- and long-term goals** that we wanted to achieve. We'd use these goals to show upper management a clear plan. The first set of goals is essentially a timetable for getting the necessary cooperation and getting things done. **By the end of the first month,** we wanted to have the plans done about equipment and facilities. **By the end of the second month,** we wanted to make sure we had all the financials back from the accounting department, and so on. We didn't think trying to decide what kind of equipment to buy was the most important thing, though. We wanted to make sure that we could demonstrate to upper management that their **money wouldn't be wasted.** So, we set up a subscription drive before we went into construction. We wanted to make sure we could demonstrate a continuing base of users. We formulated a plan to **offer** something like a free fitness evaluation for the first 100 people who signed up. We'd have*

other offers like this to **attract users and keep the facility at peak usage.**
Once we could prove that the center would be used, everything else would follow. To sell the center, we also set some **long-term financial goals,** *so we thought we'd commission a* **benefits study.** *For example, we want to document a percentage decrease in the number of sick days taken. We also want to show a direct correlation between the type of equipment we would buy and the type of health benefits.*

We also want to stick with free weights and Nautilus equipment, and other equipment that was tied into improving the cardiovascular system and relieving stress. We'd let upper management know that **not building a fitness center would mean continued low morale, lowered productivity, and higher insurance costs.**

How many goals did you stress in your Fitness Center strategy? Did you compare benefits with the consequences of not building the facility? Or is your report completely different?

Influence Exercise 13: The Compelling Style

Now that you're familiar with the Compelling style of influence, complete Exercise 13 to test your understanding and identify one or more people you know who are typical of this style. Here's a summary of the characteristics of the Compelling style. The Compeller/Pragmatist:

- Offers rewards.
- Uses higher authority.
- Bargains, negotiates.
- States goals and expectations.
- Threatens consequences of noncompliance.

Influence Exercise 13: The Compelling Style

To test your understanding of the Compelling style, see how many of the characteristics of this style you can recall.

Characteristics of the style:

1. _____
2. _____
3. _____
4. _____

Person(s) I know who use this style:

1. _____
2. _____
3. _____
4. _____

Examples of their behavior:

1. _____
2. _____
3. _____
4. _____

Strengths of the Compelling style:

1. _____
2. _____
3. _____
4. _____

Weaknesses of the Compelling style:

1. _____
2. _____
3. _____
4. _____

7

Secret #3: The Felling/ Preservationist Style

If you scored high in the third column of your inventory score sheet in Chapter 4, then you primarily use the Felling strategy. The hallmark of the Felling style is the attempt to gain influence or power by "winning" over others.

Doing It the Tried and True Way

A good example of a Feller is a bureaucrat, someone who sticks to a position and attempts to gain influence or power by remaining firm. Another type of Feller is a good attorney who carefully cross-examines a witness and extracts only the information that is helpful.

Timberrrr!

I named this style Felling (as when foresters "fell" trees) because people who use it tend to "fell" (cut down) the ideas of others. While it can be useful when the ideas are indeed "blue sky," crazy, or impractical, Fell-

ing used too early in the decision-making process can sometimes nip po-
tentially good ideas in the bud, before they've had a chance to develop
in any way. Fellers would never have backed Columbus' idea about sail-
ing the Atlantic!

Typically, Felling is used when another person presents ideas or proposals that are in opposition to yours, or seem unrealistic or unfeasible.
Like Telling, this style uses logic and reason to influence. Unlike Telling, however, Felling's main focus is *reactive*, using logic to counter others' ideas. People who use this style can wield facts persuasively. They
are good at setting priorities and minimizing risks. They can hold firm
and stick to a position. They are also able to grasp inconsistencies in a
situation.

The disadvantages of the Felling style are a lack of flexibility and difficulty in picking up the subtle cues in a situation. A Feller is a Preservationist. Users of this style value tradition and the status quo, and they
tend to be impatient with seemingly impractical ideas that threaten to
"rock the boat." As logical as they like to think they are, their reasoning
can break down as the result of a faulty assumption—that something
should continue as it is purely because it has traditionally existed or
been done that way.

Felling is most effective when others are looking to you for expertise,
"reality" testing, and as mentioned, when ideas being presented might
be unrealistic or unfeasible. It can be ineffective when ideas are new,
still in the "budding" or developmental stages, and need a sympathetic
hearing.

Listening for "Felling" Words

You can tell when people are using Felling by the kind of language they
use. You may hear statements such as "We've never done this before" or
"We've always done it the other way, why change now?" Words like *tradition, maintain,* and *continue* are likely to make Fellers feel more secure than words like *new, innovative, hunch,* or *gut feeling.* Later on in
this book, we'll discuss techniques for dealing successfully with people
who use this style.

If you are primarily a Feller, the Influence Styles Inventory statements you checked included:

- I'll point out flaws, mistakes, or inconsistencies in the proposals or
ideas of others.
- I'll challenge an idea that won't work.
- When someone presents a "blue sky" idea, I bring them back to reality.

■ I can quickly zero in on people's mistaken assumptions.

The attitudes of Fellers are also revealed in the words and expressions they use, as in the following examples:

"We must *maintain* the existing fitness center facility."

"Let's make sure that our ideas *aren't too far out*."

"But we *have always used*...so why change now?"

"We *can't* afford to *experiment*."

In order to recognize your own influence style—or the style of someone trying to influence you—it is helpful to be able to "hear" it. Again, as pointed out throughout this book, listen for the influence style and learn to hear it in yourself and in others.

Felling in Action

The following account offers an example of Felling used to influence upper management to set up an in-house fitness center. Pay particular attention to the **boldface italic** words and phrases. The strategy here is markedly different from those presented in the other chapters on influence styles, though the goal is of course the same. Which style is the best to reach this goal? The answer depends not only on personalities in upper management and the nature of the company itself, but also on the proposer's ability to use the chosen style well.

The Fitness Center
The Felling Point of View

*We thought the best approach was to find a company that **already had a fitness center** and use that as a model to convince upper management. We would list **all the companies** that were putting in fitness centers, and why for them it **wasn't such a radical idea**. Our plan stresses that we wouldn't be able to **maintain** our competitiveness if we didn't have one. The best way to convince upper management is to **use another company like ours as a model**. We think it would be an easier sell if we simply **duplicated a successful facility**.*

*We also thought that the best way of constructing a presentation is to make sure that we can answer everyone's objections, so we thought that we'd talk to some key people informally to see what **objections they would have to the center**. We also want to be able to answer people who want to be **too innovative** because we don't think upper management would go for the latest facili-*

*ties. We think the key is to be **careful, and not try to rock the boat** and just present **what has worked before, what has already proved itself**.*

   Is your strategy conservative? Do you want to make sure you can answer everybody's questions? This is certainly one way of approaching the problem of making your influence felt.

Influence Exercise 14:
The Felling Style

Now that you're familiar with the Felling style of influence, complete Exercise 14 to test your understanding and identify one or more people you know who are typical Fellers. Here's a summary of the characteristics of the Felling style. A Feller/Preservationist:

- Points out flaws or inconsistencies in others' ideas.
- Challenges ideas as unworkable.
- Maintains the status quo.
- Holds firm to his or her position.

Influence Exercise 14: The Felling Style

Now see how many of the characteristics of this style you recall.

Characteristics of the style:

1. _____

2. _____

3. _____

4. _____

Person(s) I know who use this style:

1. _____

2. _____

3. _____

4. _____

5. _____

Examples of their behavior:

1. _____

2. _____

3. _____

4. _____

Strengths of the Felling style:

1. _____

2. _____

3. _____

4. _____

Weaknesses of the Felling style:

1. _____

2. _____

3. _____

4. _____

8
Secret #4:
The Welling/
Catalyst Style

If you scored high in the fourth column of the inventory score sheet in Chapter 4, you are primarily a Weller. The name for the Welling style comes from the idea of a well, a deep source of supply. Wellers are seen that way by others.

Doing It Heart to Heart

Welling is characterized by the ability to gain rapport easily with others. Some people can naturally or intuitively establish a rapport with other people and win their trust; others must learn. Welling can be a powerful influence strategy if it is used sincerely and if you are genuinely interested in understanding and empathizing with others. Establishing a rapport—a relationship based on mutual trust and shared feelings—can be accomplished by:

- Disclosing one's own feelings (positive and negative) to others.
- Being loyal.
- Keeping confidences.
- Supporting others' ideas, feelings, and projects.

Rapport can be established in form as well. The important thing is that the other person feels—has a sense—that you are in harmony or "in sync" with him or her.

People who use the Welling style listen attentively, eliciting contributions from others and showing understanding and appreciation. They focus on the strengths of others' ideas and resources rather than pushing their own, and they give credit to others when it's due. They are seen as supportive, open, and flexible. This style is characterized by "pulling" others into your sphere of influence, rather than "pushing" them to do what you want.

Wellers trade off close control of behavior for higher commitment on the part of the other person. That's why we also think of Welling as the style of the catalyst — in the sense of someone who gets others to motivate themselves and do the job expected of them.

Because Welling is, in many ways, a minimodel or microcosm of all seven secrets of influence, it warrants a more elaborate discussion to help you to understand not only this particular style, but what the entire book is all about.

Welling to Succeed

Welling is most effective when:

- A high-quality solution depends on the pooling of resources, and all or almost all of those involved have something to contribute which is necessary for the desired outcome.

- Commitment to carrying out a course of action is essential to its success, and that commitment cannot simply be compelled (for example, the situation in which a number of managers of equal rank but of different functions must agree to carry out a plan).

- The other person has important knowledge and skills that you do not possess and may not even know enough to evaluate. This is often the case when managing specialists, professionals, or scientific personnel. In these cases you do not have the knowledge base for directing precisely the behavior required, and so you must fall back upon establishing commitment to overall objectives.

- The person or team being managed is highly resistant to being controlled or persuaded and perhaps has a great personal or professional need.

It is important to know the limitations of each style. Welling may be ineffective in certain situations; for instance, when:

- The speed of decision and action is more important than the quality of the decision — when perfectionism shouldn't inhibit progress.

- You are uniquely qualified to decide and no deep commitment on the part of others is required to carry out the decision effectively.

- It is not in the other person's best interest to cooperate, or this person perceives cooperation with you as weakening his or her competitive situation.

To succeed with Welling, you must recognize those situations in which it will indeed work for you.

The Right Personal Touch

You may know someone who is a good listener, establishes close relationships with others easily, and isn't shy about revealing personal matters. Chances are this person is a Weller. Wellers don't think of themselves as particularly powerful. Often, by acting as catalysts, they are the power behind the power. By making others seem powerful and visible, they tend to wield more influence than they realize.

The Weller demonstrates an honesty in dealing with people. If you are a Weller, you're probably people-oriented, preferring to be part of a group rather than to work alone on a project. You value personal relationships and human stories. You chat with coworkers. You like to form intimate connections with others and to get to know them in all their facets, not just their work sides. You relish the give-and-take of sharing others' ideas and perspectives. You're likely to appear warm, supportive, flexible, and empathetic, and you use Welling statements such as "I know what you mean" or "That happened to me once, too."

Even with relative strangers, you establish rapport easily. How can you tell you've got rapport? Sometimes you simply feel it, but often, they tell you: "You're very much like me," "We're in sync," or "It's nice to talk to someone who speaks my language...is on my wavelength...knows where I'm coming from...." People may even tell you that they trust you or feel you understand them even when you don't agree with everything they say.

Sometimes you use other influence styles, different approaches, and even different language (slang, jargon, etc.), depending on whom you're working with. You may worry, though, that you're not firm enough, that perhaps you're too easily swayed or too much of a chameleon. You may even be haunted by the notion frequently expressed that "Nice guys finish last," while at the same time you refuse to accept such a cynical dog-eat-dog credo.

For those who are Wellers, you're probably quite good at gathering lots of information from others, factual data as well as intuitive impressions. You like to get to the heart of things. You don't like brief summaries or mere statements of fact—you find them too thin and dry, and wish that people who present them would add more life, more flesh, because you need a more complete picture. The bare bones approach is definitely not for you.

Watching for Wellers

Now that you know some of the attributes of the Welling style, you can look for them in other people. You'll discover all kinds of things that you may have never noticed before. You may, for example, have colleagues who prefer face-to-face meetings rather than inanimate, fact-filled memos. When they are given the concise bottom line, they usually want more elaboration and explanation. They are probably comfortable expressing their own personal feelings or beliefs to you and appear to be warm, caring individuals.

To communicate with them — and influence them — you have to show Wellers that you value human interaction by demonstrating warmth, openness, and flexibility. Later in this chapter, you'll learn some specific techniques that you can use to communicate more effectively with Wellers.

When Welling Works

The Welling style can work with groups as well as one-on-one. It's especially useful for people in upper management.

Welling in a Team Setting

Since Welling involves pulling others into your circle of influence in order to establish collaborative working relationships, it can be very effective when commitment to a group effort is important. If, for example, you need to recruit volunteers to work with you on a two-year task force, Welling might prove to be an effective approach. Welling is especially useful in working with people who have different needs or goals and who may have equally different skills and contributions.

Influence Scenario 3

A Model Weller

One of the most effective Wellers I've known worked in the computer area at AT&T. He had a marvelous method for gaining input from others while still setting forth his own solution. When he

needed to call a brainstorming session, he sent a memo to each of
the attendees in advance, inviting their ideas on some matter. He
would request that their suggestions be given to him in writing prior
to the meeting. He never indicated that he already had some
possible ideas for a solution. When the people came to the meeting,
he asked each of them to elaborate on his or her idea. He would
listen carefully. When one person was talking, he silently observed
the others' reactions, noting their nonverbal signals of support or
rejection. As a Weller, he's good at reading body language. By the
time the last person spoke, he had completed his "silent ballot" — he
knew which ideas were likely to be supported. Then, he carefully
presented his idea, weaving into it the best suggestions from each
member of the group.

I have seen him use this method with many different people. He
demonstrated both *attentiveness* — really listening and paying attention
to other people's thoughts, needs, and hidden agendas — and *flexibility* — shaping his own idea so it was ultimately in tune with those of the
other group members.

It is also significant that he seemed not to have a large investment in
claiming ownership of the idea, and often other members of the group
got the credit for what turned out to be the winning solution, even
though it had been his plan all along.

Welling One-on-One

If you're dealing with only one person, Welling can still be useful, especially if the other person has important knowledge, skills, or resources that you don't have. Say, for example, that you're the manager
of several technical professionals. You may not necessarily be an expert
in the technical aspects of your field, but as manager, you are responsible for seeing that overall goals are achieved. It would be particularly
helpful for you to use the pulling-together approach of the Welling
style, gathering information as you go, without imposing or pushing
your ideas.

In his recent book *High Output Management*, Andrew Grove, former
chairman of Intel, discloses a diary of his activities over the course of
several days. A great percentage of those activities were assigned to a
category which he called "data gathering." These activities took various
forms: attending meetings; listening to one of his vice presidents; reading reports from customers; and so forth. He, and others in similar positions of authority, believes in the power of tuning in to others. They
have learned how to lead — how to influence — by listening.

Welling can also be the solution when another person resists being
controlled or being told what to do. One manager I know, an on-the-

rise employee of a medium-sized manufacturing company, made a classic mistake. After being promoted to head a department where among those he was to supervise were two coworkers who had also been considered for the job, the new manager decided to run his department using the Telling style, detailing his whole approach to the situation and assuming that it would be the way things would work. Not surprisingly, he met with strong resistance when he tried to dictate to his former peers what he wanted done, how he wanted it done, and by when. After exposure to the full range of influence styles, he realized that he would be much more successful in his new position by encouraging input and ideas from those directly under him. He returned to his company and leveled with his coworkers: he let them know that he had made a mistake by being too bossy, too dictatorial, and that he really wanted to have a good working relationship with them. Most people have a hard time using authority well under any conditions, and in this situation in particular, the collaborative, indirect management style was ultimately better for engendering cooperation and productivity.

Welling at the Top

Wellers are often found in top management where many people with different personal and professional goals must be united to accomplish the organization's mission. Senior executives are not always Wellers on their way to the top, but once there, many find it is the most effective style for upper management. Wellers are also often found in jobs such as sales, in which it is of paramount importance to identify a client's needs and wants in order to make the sale. Wellers also work in staff jobs such as administrative services and human resources (personnel) where they give other people and departments the support they need.

When Welling Doesn't Work

The Welling style usually requires time and patience. It isn't the approach to use when you need fast action or quick decisions. If the building is on fire and you're the only one who knows where the exits are, you should obviously use a more direct approach than Welling!

I once hired an outside consultant to write a training manual because my company needed the project done *fast*. Despite the fact that she had direct experience in the field and I'd given her plenty of notes, she wanted to spend two or three days with me "getting my input" on the manual. Had I spent the two or three days in the Welling style she preferred, we would have missed our deadline.

Furthermore, if you're the only person who has the resources or information needed to make a decision, then you may be placing an unfair burden on others by expecting them to contribute to the decision-making process. This approach could also reflect negatively on you, as it may suggest that you are abdicating your responsibilities, that is, just passing the buck.

How to Be a Better Weller

The most important characteristic of the Welling style is that Wellers can establish rapport easily. They do this primarily by listening—by tuning in to other people. While this may seem quite basic, passive, and not necessarily powerful, you'll soon see how it can be a valuable tool for proactively influencing others.

Working Well with Wellers

Be a "People" Person

If the person you're trying to influence is a Weller, he or she enjoys and appreciates the art of listening, likes to get to know others on a personal basis, and often will be quite flexible. People like this (and you may be one) often weave personal stories into a business conversation, and they like to find out about you. They often like working in groups, teams, and task forces, not only for the creative synergy with others, but also for the sheer enjoyment they get from being around other people. They are, in a word, gregarious. When you're dealing with a Weller (and of course, you'll find this easier if you're one, too), it's important to be aware of these preferences and ways of working.

Give Them Time to Warm Up

If you're trying to influence Wellers by showing them the cost-benefit ratio of a plan you have, you'll probably do better to open up with some small talk, find out how their day is going, and talk briefly about some nonbusiness topics. You may find this "off purpose" or a waste of time, but it's absolutely necessary to do this warmup with a Weller. Nothing lengthy is required, but Wellers prefer some time for both people to feel comfortable with each other—*first* as people, then as coworkers.

Solicit Their Participation

If you are approaching a Weller and have your idea all thought out, typed, and ready to present, you should rethink this modus operandi. Give Wellers some opportunity to "play." If you are just coming to them with the bottom line, you may be seen as denying them the chance to involve themselves, to collaborate. You may also be denying yourself some good advice—Wellers tend to be good at what they do.

Remember, too, that Wellers are often more interested in the *process* than in the outcome of the day-to-day affairs of business.

Influence Scenario 4

Getting There Is Half the Fun

My friend Joseph, the personnel manager for a large retail department store, described for me a new performance appraisal system his personnel group had been working on. Did he tell me the details of the forms, and the different aspects of employee performance this system would evaluate? No. First he told me about the off-site meeting the whole group had had and how nicely everyone related to one another. He was proud—in human terms—of the way his group had performed. The fact that they emerged with a great system was of course important too, but he put a special value on having assembled a strong group that worked well together.

Listening for "Welling" Words

Listening is key to the success of the Welling style. It is also a skill that plays an important role in the ultimate success of all influence styles.

If you're primarily a Weller, some of the inventory statements you checked included:

- I often change my ideas after hearing the opinions of others.

- When presenting my ideas, I actively encourage the suggestions and ideas of others.

- My communication style can change considerably, depending on whom I'm talking to.

- I'll readily admit my lack of expertise when I'm trying to influence others.

These statements can be rephrased as questions and then asked of people you want to influence in order to find out if you're dealing with a Weller.

You can also listen for Welling words that reveal the style:

"We will *survey* employees to get their input into how the center should be decided."

"We need some *mutually agreed upon* ground rules for use of the center."

"*Before* we get down to *business*, I want to mention that you seem kind of down lately. Is there *anything I can do*?"

Welling in Action

Now here's an account that demonstrates how a planning group approaches selling the fitness center idea to upper management by using the Welling style. The **boldface italic** phrases are typical of Wellers.

The Fitness Center
The Welling Point of View

*The first thing we thought we would do is to conduct a **user survey**. We'd want to find out what kind of facilities everyone would want. We'd work with the human resources committee to **formulate the survey**. We'd then put together some sort of **employee committee** to help us go over the surveys and come up with concrete recommendations. We'd try to **include** people who belong to health clubs on this committee. At this meeting, we'd present a **couple of variations** suggested by the survey results. We'd also do some separate **consulting** with the building management people and someone who runs a local gym for **some input**. We also think it would be a good idea to try to have the gym **affiliated** with a chain of some kind, like Jack LaLanne, so it would be easier to operate. We don't think we should present a finished facilities plan to upper management. We'd suggest some outline and **work with upper management** to develop the ultimate plan. This way, if they get to **give us their input**, it would be easier for us to get them to buy into the fitness center idea. Of course we'll try to encourage their support in terms of how the fitness center will help the company by **helping the people who are the company**.*

Did your fitness center plan sound anything like this one? Did your strategy involve getting other people actively to contribute to the plan and have a big hand in the final decision?

Influence Exercise 15:
The Welling Style

Now that you're acquainted with the Welling style of influence, you can test your understanding and identify one or more people you know who are typical of this style. Here is a summary of the characteristics of the Welling style. The Weller/Catalyst:

- Is flexible; changes after hearing others' ideas.
- Actively encourages others' suggestions.
- Actively listens to both verbal and nonverbal cues.
- Accurately rephrases.
- Uses self-disclosure.
- Elaborates.

Influence Exercise 15: The Welling Style

Now see how many of the characteristics of the Welling style you recall.

Characteristics of the style:

1. _____

2. _____

3. _____

4. _____

5. _____

6. _____

Person(s) I know who use this style:

1. _____

2. _____

3. _____

4. _____

5. _____

Examples of their behavior:

1. _____

2. _____

3. _____

(Continued)

4. _____

5. _____

Strengths of the Welling style:

1. _____

2. _____

3. _____

4. _____

Weaknesses of the Welling style:

1. _____

2. _____

3. _____

4. _____

9

Secret #5:
The Selling/
Strategist Style

Perhaps you had your highest score in the fifth column of the Influence Styles Inventory score sheet in Chapter 4. If so, you primarily use the Selling style. Selling is the style of the strategist.

Doing It like an Artist

The Selling style must be both artful and hopeful to work well. This style combines some of the skills of the other styles, such as Welling (gaining rapport), Telling (articulate presentation of one's ideas), and Gelling (creating a common vision or shared purpose). It also includes astute listening to how the other person says things (form) as well as to what is actually said (content).

People who are effective Sellers ask probing questions early in the influencing process, in order to determine the other's underlying needs and motivations as well as learn his or her preferred form of communication. Sellers listen to the tone and the words of the other's communication and tailor theirs to match in terms of word choice and figures of speech. They also ask questions that "qualify the prospect," to find out how likely he or she is to resist their offer or suggestions. Once rapport and trust have been established, Sellers present their ideas so that they appeal to the prospect and offer benefits tailored specifically to that person's needs and motivations. Users of this style get long-term commitments by getting agreement to small chunks of their proposals, and they test the waters frequently in order to gauge their progress in the influence process.

When they encounter resistance, Sellers pay careful attention to its form and meaning, concede its possible validity, and continue to demonstrate the value of their proposals by helping the "influencee" overcome his or her blocks, real or imagined, to saying yes.

Finally, they pay special attention to the decision strategies of others, and when the time is right to close, they present the proposition in the most appropriate sequence and form. Using the "assumptive" close — assuming the other will ultimately "buy" — they phrase the close in positive language, similar to personalized language used in the rapport-building phase.

The Selling style is most effective when dealing with multiple stakeholders and issues, for example, when individuals in a group all have different goals or differ on issues. It can be ineffective when there is no opportunity for personal contact or for reading signals or nonverbal cues about the other person.

Listening for "Selling" Words

The ability to use language artfully is the hallmark of good Sellers. To be able to speak the same language spoken by the person to be influenced is key to the success of the Selling style — whether that language is the language of big business, the street, the ivory tower, the bottom line, or even a foreign culture like Japan.

If you are a Seller, you probably checked the following statements in the Influence Style Inventory:

- I always tell people specifically how my ideas benefit them.
- I try to discover what motivates each person when I'm trying to influence others.
- I'm satisfied when people agree to only a piece of what I'm proposing.
- When trying to influence others, I take the time to figure out people's individual decision-making styles.

These statements demonstrate how Selling involves making basic discoveries about targeted "buyers" of ideas and how Sellers base their optimistic strategies on these discoveries. The point is, sharp language skills are often what makes these essential discoveries possible in the first place.

So, how can you buzz the words that sell? Or how can you identify them in the language of a Seller? The few examples that follow show you how the Selling style manifests itself verbally:

"The *needs* of our employees dictate that..."

"The *benefits* to be derived from such a facility include..."

"*Your goals* can surely be *achieved*..."

Selling in Action

Here is how a Selling team might present its fitness center to influence top management. Sellers use words and phrases like the ones **boldfaced** in the plan.

The Fitness Center
The Selling Point of View

*We like the idea of finding out how other companies did it, but we don't think that what's in the gym is that important. We can always decide that later. We thought it'd be best to find out how other companies' employees sold the idea internally. We thought the best idea was first to sell the idea, then decide on the particulars. Our survey would be one to find out what the users would need, without telling them what we were doing so the sample would be pure. For instance, we would ask them **about their workload**. If they said they **felt they were overworked**, then it would be clearly demonstrable that a health facility **would help them relieve the tension** that being overworked invariably creates. If people **thought they were too isolated**, then we could sell the concept of the facility as a place where **people would get together**—not just for workouts but for shop talk as well (a lot of big corporate decisions happen in the locker room).*

*We'd try to link the costs with savings in health insurance premiums and increased productivity. But we'd also stress that there are **gains beyond money**, like happy employees who do more work because they're happy. These are **benefits** that can't be put on a balance sheet. We also think it would be easier to sell upper management in **stages**. First, we'd suggest that before building our own facility, we'd get some sort of agreement with a local health club that would allow our employees use of their facilities at a greatly reduced cost. We could then see how many people would use it, and what the **benefits** are. The we'd build a small facility for one division **to see how it worked out in-house**.*

How much of a sell job do you think this project is? Did you think in terms of selling the concept or coming up with a whole new proposal?

Influence Exercise 16:
The Selling Style

Now that you're familiar with the Selling style of influence, complete Exercise 16 to test your understanding and identify one or more people you know who are typical of this style. Here is a summary of the characteristics of the Selling style. The Seller/Strategist:

- Presents ideas in terms of benefits to others' *specific* needs and goals (stated or implied).
- Uses small "closes" or commitments.
- Gives attention to individual decision strategy.
- Acknowledges objections and handles them.

Influence Exercise 16: The Selling Style

See how many of the characteristics of the Selling style you can recall.

Characteristics of the style:

1. _____

2. _____

3. _____

4. _____

Person(s) I know who use this style:

1. _____

2. _____

3. _____

4. _____

Examples of their behavior:

1. _____

2. _____

3. _____

4. _____

5. _____

Strengths of the Selling style:

1. _____

2. _____

3. _____

4. _____

Weaknesses of the Selling style:

1. _____

2. _____

3. _____

4. _____

10
Secret #6: The Gelling/ Idealist Style

If your marks fell mostly in the sixth column of the Influence Styles Inventory in Chapter 4, then you use the Gelling strategy. When two or more people's ideas come together to form a single vibrant entity, it is a figure of speech to say that these ideas are "gelling"; hence the name for this particular style of influence.

Doing It with Vision

As a way to influence, Gelling involves identifying and articulating a common or shared vision of what the future of an organization, group, or individual could be and strengthening others' beliefs that the desired outcome can be achieved through their individual and collective efforts. People who use the Gelling style mobilize the energy and resources of others by appealing to their hopes, values, and aspirations. They also activate the feelings of strength and confidence that are generated by being one of a large group that shares a common purpose.

Gelling requires the ability to present ideas powerfully—but its appeal is not so much to the intellect as it is to the emotions and values of the others involved. The Geller attempts to develop enthusiasm for aspirations and ideals and to channel that energy into work and problem solving, usually in a group or team.

Big Chiefs Have Big Dreams

People who use the Gelling style are able to see and articulate to others the exciting possibilities that exist in an idea or project and to project those possibilities enthusiastically. This approach implies a future orientation, and the skilled practitioner uses images that kindle excitement about a better future which *the listeners value*. A good Geller also helps people identify their values, hopes, and aspirations (individually, and those they hold in common).

Gellers use exciting images and figures of speech to communicate their messages, and they are often very colorful in their use of language. They are *idealists* who paint a picture of a brighter future. They speak in language that resonates and strikes a deep chord in us all.

When Gelling Works Best

When used appropriately, Gelling can be a most powerful style of influence. In some ways it is a more specialized influence style than the others. It has great power in a range of situations:

- When values, aspirations, and interests are common to you and those you want to influence; that is, situations in which you want or need to activate values rather than to change them.

- When you have qualities that make it easy for the people you want to influence to identify with you; in other words, you are the kind of person the others would like to become (a role model), but you are not so different from them that identification with you is difficult or farfetched.

- When the other person is not entirely sure what he or she wants to do or how to solve his or her problems; situations in which the other person is dissatisfied with the status quo and looking for direction and guidance.

- When taking decisive action is less important than others' lending commitment and energy to a chosen course; also, situations in which a general and new direction is not required, but a higher level of commitment, effort, and energy is needed for an existing objective.

- When important fears, hopes, and values have recently been aroused by events or personal experience; situations in which people are concerned about something in common. The influencer's function here would be to accentuate the common interests and goals of the group and channel its energy into work on a task or into conflict with some external group, situation, or idea.

- You're in an "underdog" or turnaround situation in which you must influence others to believe that the seemingly impossible can be accomplished and motivate them to extraordinary achievement in a relatively short time.

If you have low prestige and status compared to the people you want to influence, you may make effective use of this influence style by finding your common ground.

Gelling is the style of influence used by great orators such as Martin Luther King. In his "I Have a Dream" speech, King demonstrated the power of Gelling. He articulated his vision and mission in highly picturesque language that struck a lasting chord of the deepest emotions, beliefs, and values in the people he addressed—and he inspired them to join in his mission. A follower of King said it best when she said: "He spoke for all of us. He said what we had inside us—he just said it better than we could."

Gelling is most similar to what is referred to as "symbolic influence" in the Harvard studies mentioned in Chapter 1. It is characterized by using symbols of group identity, such as a group slogan or insignia.

When Gelling Doesn't Work

Gelling is unlikely to be effective when you are not trusted. This may be the case when you are identified with a group believed to be opposed to the goals and interests of the person or persons you are trying to influence. Gelling should not be employed as an influencing strategy when rapport and trust have not been established or when quick solutions are needed.

Listening for "Gelling" Words

If you are a Geller, some of the statements that you probably chose from the Influence Styles Inventory are:

- I present my ideas by appealing to emotions, not logic.
- I get others to act by establishing a shared mission.
- When I'm trying to influence people, I appeal to their dreams and ideals.
- In selling my ideas, I use images and metaphors of a better future.

Some words and phrases common to the Gelling style are:

- "Our *vision* of this new facility is…"
- "The *possibilities* of a fitness center are endless."
- "We'll have *fun!*"

Gelling in Action

Let's tune in to the strategy meeting of a Gelling team describing its fitness center. Gellers use words and phrases similar to those in **boldfaced** type.

The Fitness Center
The Gelling Point of View

*We thought the best way to sell the idea is to show upper management a **beforeand-after picture**—here we have scrawny, unhappy, and sickly employees who come to work, do their jobs, and go home. We'd compare this with an "after" picture—dynamic, healthy, and happy employees who are energetic, motivated, and highly productive. We'd stress the **old proverb** about how a healthy body leads to a healthy mind. Our employees could all look and feel like **Wonder Woman or Superman**. Their personal vivacious quality would be transferred to the company as a whole. In order to accomplish this **vision**, we see an **innovative** gym with **state-of-the-art** equipment. We want to make sure that we don't do anything halfway, since we feel that doing the gym that way would never accomplish our ultimate goal. **If we do it at all, we're going to do it right**. We want all employees to tap into their **inner greatness**, to help **catapult** productivity to new levels. You can't do this by having old equipment or the same facilities as everyone else. Once we present this **vision**, it would be easier to present the particulars. After all, the big chiefs have **the big dreams**—that's how great things begin, with gutsy great ideas, like **the American Dream**!*

Did you use metaphors and hyperbole of a grand future vision as part of your strategy? If so, it indicates your tendency toward the Gelling style of influence.

Influence Exercise 17:
The Gelling Style

Now that you're familiar with the Gelling style of influence, complete Exercise 17 to test your understanding and identify one or more people you know who are typical of this style. Here is a summary of the characteristics of the Gelling style. The Geller/Idealist:

- Uses emotions rather than logic.
- Promotes a shared mission, common vision.
- Has a future orientation.
- Employs images and metaphors.

Influence Exercise 17: The Gelling Style

See how many of the characteristics of this style you recall.

Characteristics of the style:

1. _____

2. _____

3. _____

4. _____

Person(s) I know who use this style:

1. _____

2. _____

3. _____

4. _____

Examples of their behavior:

1. _____

2. _____

3. _____

4. _____

Strengths of the Gelling style:

1. _____

2. _____

3. _____

4. _____

Weaknesses of the Gelling style:

1. _____

2. _____

3. _____

4. _____

11
The Six Influence Styles: A Summary and Review

You have just finished learning about the six styles of influence. Here's a brief summary of each style's characteristics.

The Teller/Analyst:

Prefers logic to emotion.
Justifies arguments or ideas with reasons and evidence.
Values structure and organization.
Likes to integrate and link into others' points.
Is inclined to elaborate on positions.

The Compeller/Pragmatist:

Offers rewards.
Uses higher authority.
Bargains, negotiates.
States goals and expectations.
Threatens consequences of noncompliance.

The Feller/Preservationist:

Points out flaws or inconsistencies in others' ideas.
Challenges ideas as unworkable.
Maintains the status quo.
Holds firm to his or her position.

The Weller/Catalyst: Is flexible; changes after hearing others' ideas.
Actively encourages others' suggestions.
Actively listens to both verbal and nonverbal cues.
Accurately rephrases.
Uses self-disclosure.
Elaborates.

The Seller/Strategist: Presents ideas in terms of benefits to others' *specific* needs and goals (stated or implied).
Uses small "closes" or commitments.
Gives attention to individual decision strategy.
Acknowledges objections and handles them.

The Geller/Idealist: Uses emotions rather than logic.
Promotes shared, or common, vision.
Has future orientation.
Employs vivid language, images, and metaphors.

Your objective is now to learn how you can use your self-knowledge to understand others better and to influence them more easily.

Influencing the Teller/Analyst

Because Tellers are so fact-oriented, they might like some *statistics* to back up your assertions or requests. They certainly would appreciate a *rational* discussion of any issues involved, and they care a lot about *substance*. "Where's the beef?" or "What's the point?" are Teller types of questions, especially if they feel they are just getting "fluff" or a peripheral discussion. Tellers want facts, but they want them in a logical, structured way. At the beginning of a presentation, Tellers want to know what the *procedures* and *ground rules* are. They don't like surprises.

The Teller Unpersuaded

What would a Teller *not* like, if you were presenting something or trying to influence? You can leave out *assumptions* that are vague or fuzzy, since the Teller only wants crisp, provable facts. What's more, a long-winded discussion of your personal ideals, emotions, and beliefs would probably fall on deaf ears if you were trying to persuade a Teller. Such an approach might even make them uncomfortable, since they don't believe that emotional talk has any place in business. Tellers also feel uncomfortable in ambiguous or unstructured situations. If you're having a meeting with a Teller, make sure *you* plan it carefully ahead of time, with an agenda and clearly defined objectives.

Influencing the Compeller/Pragmatist

If you are making a presentation to a person who prefers the Compelling style of influence, what are some things this person might like? Compellers want to know what rewards are in store if they agree to what you are proposing. They also want to know the negative consequences. A Compeller welcomes good negotiation and bargaining as part of the influencing process. He or she probably would like to hear case examples of past negotiations that might be similar to the present situation, and how they came out. Compelling is the style of the *Pragmatist*, so a Compeller is very results-oriented. A clear statement of objectives, standards, measurements, and long-range plans all will contribute to a Compeller's feeling comfortable with you.

The Compeller Unpersuaded

Now, what might a Compeller dislike? Compellers are very motivated by rewards, so if they perceive that there are no rewards or not very clearly defined ones, they will not be interested in what you are offering or proposing. Since they see negotiating as a game and bargaining as a sport, if something is presented to them in absolutes, it doesn't seem very interesting or intriguing. They are practical and pragmatic, so long or theoretical discussions will go over their heads. To Compellers, this level of conversation does not seem to go anywhere. And they also dislike emotional talk. Like Tellers, they feel that it has no place in business and that bottom-line issues are the only subjects worth discussing.

Influencing the Feller/Preservationist

When you're trying to influence or persuade a Feller, remember that they value tradition. They like to know that whatever they are considering has a precedent or some basis in the past. Thus you should talk about time or a continuum, and you should show that your idea or proposal is in keeping with a historical viewpoint. It is also helpful to quote from authorities or experts, since the Feller is often impressed with this kind of support. Like Tellers, Fellers like short, direct, factual discussions of the issues. They too want to know about rules, policies, and precedents. Fellers are usually people who like to operate by the book. But, since they also like to look for flaws, it is often a good strategy to present something *with minor flaws* or inconsistencies to give them the opportunity to play at what they do best.

The Feller Unpersuaded

What turns a Feller off? Certainly, Fellers do not like long, rambling small talk. And although they may *say* they don't like impractical ideas, in a way they welcome hearing them, because it gives them the opportunity to "fell" such ideas—that is, to find their flaws and imperfections. You've already been introduced to some techniques for dealing with a Felling style when you're on the receiving end of this approach. Another good strategy is to agree with the Feller in criticism of your report, proposal, or idea. Joining with Fellers by assisting them in doing what they want to do gives them the feeling that you understand where they are coming from. The principle is: Be attentive—sense where other people are coming from—and be flexible—join them in their own style or way of operating.

Influencing the Weller/Catalyst

We also practiced the Welling style of influence, the style of the *Catalyst*. What are some of the preferences of the Weller? Of course, since Wellers value relationships, they often welcome a human interest story from you, especially if it is relevant to the business under discussion. With Wellers, results are accomplished by adding a human dimension to the work relationship. They appreciate the personal touch—a little talk about your personal life, letting them in on you as a person. A Weller enjoys the give and take of ideas and even small talk, because they further the personal relationships that Wellers consider basic to business transactions.

Wellers like to listen, so you may certainly deviate somewhat from the meeting's agenda. Remember that they also like good listeners, so make sure to open your ears and give them some valuable air time. You will be rewarded, most likely, with a win-win situation, getting the results you want.

The Weller Unpersuaded

If you are planning to present something to a Weller, the bare-bones approach with just the facts will not be enough. It will appear too thin, not meaty enough. In addition, keep in mind that Wellers don't usually like to work alone because they are so gregarious and relationship-oriented. Iit is often a good idea to plan to work in a group, team, or task force.

Influencing the Seller/Strategist

More on Selling Your Way to Success

Like Gelling, Selling has rapport as its foundation. Both styles require listening (attentiveness) to other people and gaining insight into their needs, goals, motivations (their "inner" characteristics), as well as to the way they present their ideas and themselves (their influence styles, their preferred modes of presenting, and of receiving and processing information—"outer" characteristics). Of course, after rapport is achieved, you can use the appropriate influence style for the specific person and situation.

Selling combines some of the Welling skills, like gaining rapport on an intuitive level and listening, with Telling skills, such as the articulate and logical presentation of ideas. It also uses some Gelling skills—creating a common vision among them—that are explained more fully in the next chapter. This style is called Selling because its techniques closely resemble those used by a good salesperson. And in sales, the most important thing—after gaining rapport—is to learn all that can be learned about the person to whom you're selling.

Appealing to Needs

A key question most customers ask in a buying situation is, "What will this product or service do for me?" There are many ways to answer this basic question. One of the best ways to proceed is to work with an understanding of basic motivations. You may have heard of Maslow's hierarchy of needs. Abraham Maslow, commonly called the father of humanistic psychology, stated that we all have different basic needs, which serve as motivators for us.

At the very basic level, we have a need to survive, to be secure, to live in a predictable world. Beyond that, we have social needs, the need to belong to a group or family. At various times in our lives, we have needs for status, for recognition, for achievement, as well as for self-esteem and personal growth, which he called self-actualization. These needs, said Maslow, motivate our thoughts and actions. In satisfying our needs, we attain both long- and short-term goals. We can be in several different "need states" at the same time, even during the same day. If, say, you are feeling a need for achievement and recognition on the job and then get a phone call that your child is sick, you would be likely to enter the survival and security need state.

In selling, it is of prime importance to learn all you can about the person you're trying to influence, in terms of what their primary need "motivator" is. For example, to someone whose prime need is security, you would be wise to present your idea in terms of its solidity and predictability. To someone primarily motivated by achievement, you would present your proposal as a challenge and a growth opportunity.

In order to sell or to pitch an idea or concept to the customer's primary need, a salesperson presents ideas in terms of specific features and benefits. *Features* are the objective attributes or characteristics of an object or idea. For example, a feature of a car may be high mileage per gallon. *Benefits* are what someone accrues because of the feature. A benefit of high mileage per gallon is that it saves money. So a person selling cars would quickly identify what features are important to a customer by asking questions. By establishing rapport and observing the customer, a salesperson learns which benefits to emphasize. Saving money may not be the benefit most likely to sell the car. Perhaps the client is more concerned about the car's luxuries or design. The feature, then, is a simple, objective statement of fact. A benefit usually constitutes the answer to the question, "What will that feature do for me?"

Influence Exercise 18: Using the Right Approach to Selling

To explore more fully the concept of features and benefits, look at Exercise 18. This exercise involves four selling objectives: a car; a home

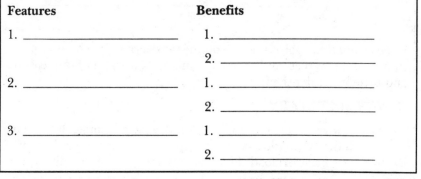

Influence Exercise 18: Selling on Features and Benefits

A. CAR

Let's start with the car. As already noted, one feature of a car is mileage. Take a few minutes to think of three or four other features you could use to sell a car. Use the space provided to list additional features.

Features   Benefits

1. _____   1. _____
                                   2. _____

2. _____   1. _____
                                   2. _____

3. _____   1. _____
                                   2. _____

(Continued)

Did you list the *size* of a car—say, compact versus full size? How *safe*
the car is? How *powerful*? Standard features like *automatic transmis-
sion*? How about *styling*? It could be a sports car or a station wagon,
for example. Or did you list some other features?

Now let's convert features into benefits. For instance, if you listed
size, what would be the benefit of, say, a small car? Ease of parking?
List at least one benefit for each feature you've listed.

If you mentioned size as a feature, what benefits did you list? If it
is a large car, did you say the car would be safer, or that you could fit
more people or things in it?

B. HOME COMPUTER

The second item for sale is a little tougher—a personal computer for
the home. Put yourself in the shoes of a computer salesperson. Identify and list at least three features of a personal computer for the
home, then at least two benefits for each feature. To make this task
easier, think of a specific person you'd like to sell the computer to,
someone you know fairly well. Then ask yourself, "What do I know
about the person I'm trying to sell this computer to that tells me what
benefits they'll care about?" If, for example, the person you're trying
to sell the computer to is busy, then an appealing feature would be
the computer's ability to automate tedious jobs, and a benefit would
be saving time.

Features   **Benefits**

1. _____   1. _____

                                            2. _____

2. _____   1. _____

                                            2. _____

3. _____   1. _____

                                            2. _____

Choose another object—a telephone answering machine, for instance, or a new piece of furniture—and work up a list of the features
and benefits of that item.

C. NEW SECRETARY

Now let's move on to trying to sell an idea, something a little more
ephemeral than a physical object. Imagine a person being slowly bur-
ied by his or her workload. List the features and the benefits of hir-

ing a secretary who could help to lighten the load. To make the job even tougher, assume that the person's boss is a cost-conscious Compeller. You'll have to tailor the features and benefits to suit this type of person. Take it one step at a time. First, come up with at least three features or aspects of a new secretary and list them below.

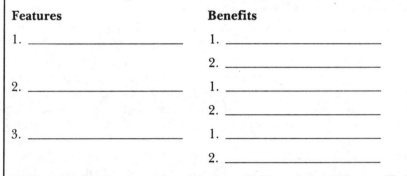

Features

1. _____

2. _____

3. _____

Benefits

1. _____

2. _____

1. _____

2. _____

1. _____

2. _____

Did you list "Help answering the phone"? How about "There will always be someone available to take care of correspondence"? Now list at least two benefits for each of the features.

What benefits did you come up with? If you had written the feature "will help answer the phones," the benefits may have been that you won't be bothered by unnecessary conversations, that having a secretary to answer the phone will enhance the image of the department, and that you'll always be sure to get your messages.

D. MOVING FROM CITY TO RURAL INDUSTRIAL PARK

If you are listing some benefits as features, or vice versa, you may want to try another example. Try selling the idea of moving your business out of the city to a rural industrial park. List three features that you'd use to convince management to make this move, and two benefits for each feature.

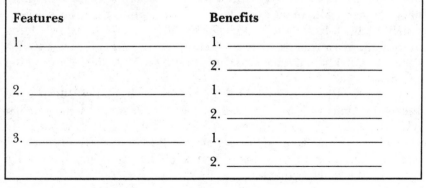

Features

1. _____

2. _____

3. _____

Benefits

1. _____

2. _____

1. _____

2. _____

1. _____

2. _____

computer; a proposal to hire a new secretary; and a proposal to move from the city to a rural industrial park. After using the everyday example of the car, you'll move on to some conceptual business issues.

Anticipating Likely Objections

As you can see, understanding features and benefits is an important part of gaining influence as a seller. When you thought about the benefits of hiring a secretary, you were probably thinking about countering objections. You may have written "less need for my working overtime" as a feature. If you did, you were anticipating an objection about costs, based on what you know about the boss. Anticipating objections is one characteristic of a good salesperson. It's a good skill to learn to become more influential.

Many people think that all they need to do is present their idea as so good, so valuable, and so irresistible that the prospect will forget all objections, and in this way they'll be able to sell their idea. But the whole concept of influence is based on selling *to* another person, not *at* them. The best way to sell to people is to anticipate their likely objections.

Whenever people tell you they are restrained by limited funds or other resources, it usually means that you haven't built up the value or benefits of what you're offering or selling, so that the cost these prospects are being asked to incur (in money, time, room, energy, or other resources) doesn't seem to be worthwhile in terms of the return they perceive they're going to get. Inexperienced sellers often get into a discussion or an argument about the price, splitting hairs and haggling over pennies. The real issue—and the key to success—is to continue to build up value so that it *outweighs* price.

It's important to acknowledge the concerns or objections people have instead of ignoring them. This way, they feel you've heard their problems and are willing to deal with them. You might say something like, "I know you mentioned last time we spoke that there wasn't much money left in your budget for the department [acknowledging objection]. With this new piece of equipment, you can save $4000 a year and quickly make back the small investment [value outweighing the price or cost]".

On the next page is a list of some common objections, "Barriers to Ideas—Roadblocks." As you read the list, you'll notice some familiar themes. This list is a useful resource for an influencer. Post a copy in your office so you can glance at it periodically when you're preparing a presentation. The list will remind you of objections to anticipate when you're in the selling situation.

Barriers to Ideas—Roadblocks

1. It's been done this way for 15 years—why change?
2. I know it won't work.
3. That's Joe's job—not mine.
4. We can't pay for the tools.
5. Cost is not important—just get it out the back door.
6. We can't help it—it's policy.
7. We don't have enough time.
8. It's not practical.
9. It costs too much.
10. That's been tried before.
11. It leaves me cold.
12. Our business is different.
13. We don't do it that way in our plant.
14. We'll come back to it later.
15. It doesn't fit in with our plans.
16. We're over the budget now.
17. Let someone else try it first.
18. They won't hold still for that.
19. It's too much trouble to change.
20. It's too late now—the contract is going to end.
21. Even if it would work, we can't qualify it.
22. We can't phase it in.
23. Nobody else has ever done it.
24. It won't work in our company.
25. The boss will never buy it.
26. The janitor says it can't be done.
27. The union will scream.
28. It's impossible.
29. There's no scheduled manpower.

Getting beyond "No"

Another skill of a Seller that can be learned is how not to take "no" for an answer. Often, when an inexperienced salesperson comes to the close or asks for the order and gets a "no," he or she quits, assuming that the person really wasn't very interested anyway. A more realistic approach is to break the large decision you're trying to get down into "bite-sized" decisions so it's easier for the prospect ultimately to say "yes" to you.

A Seller uses "no" as a starting point and works toward getting small "yes's" until the goal is achieved. The best salespeople, for instance, don't insist on all or nothing choices from a customer. Instead, they often offer a trial period, so the customer can see the item or idea in action, with no strings attached. Another version of the small "yes" is offering parts of the item or idea at a prorated price per piece, or for a trial period, or as a pilot program. In the case of hiring that secretary, instead of working for a definite "yes" or "no," you could ask your boss to hire a temporary or part-time secretary to see how having a secretary works out.

Sellers know how to get beyond "no" and gain small commitments. This is a very important skill which most good salespeople use quite naturally. You see examples of this technique all around you, in advertising for magazine subscriptions, for example, where you are offered one (or sometimes even two and three) copies of the magazine "with no obligation," and then at a later time you're invited to take a yearly subscription. In the case of book clubs, there is a powerful technique called "negative option." You are sent an order form that says you will receive that month's selection unless you take action, and you must write back and say you *don't* want the book. These marketers know that if you receive the book, glance through it, and handle it, you will probably want to keep it. You won't go through the trouble of repacking and shipping it back.

Another way you often see "small closes" in operation is in door-to-door-selling techniques. For example, you are offered a set of encyclopedias and you can pay for them one volume at a time. There once were many unscrupulous and unethical door-to-door sellers, but now the direct selling field is tightly regulated, so that it can boast some of the most socially conscious and reputable companies.

To practice scaling down your big sale, whether it's a product, idea, or proposal, write the "big yes"—the final goal—you are hoping for. Then list all the "bite-sized" steps or milestones you could use to get the small agreements which will move you toward your ultimate objective.

Tuning In to How Decisions Are Made

We all have our own processes for making decisions. For example, some people gather lots of data and information. Some get it from books in the library; some call experts in the field whom they trust; some may ask friends or relatives for advice. One person may do a detailed analysis of all the pros and cons of a particular decision. Another may use instinct and play a hunch. There are as many different processes for decision making as there are people.

One effective way to get an insight into a person's decision-making process is to see how he or she handles ordering lunch or dinner in a restaurant. One friend of mine orders the same thing (in the same diner) almost every day. Another friend waits until everyone at the table has ordered and then decides. A third friend decides very quickly, then asks the waiter for the chef's suggestion and changes her mind. Ask someone you know, "How did you decide to buy your last car?" If you listen closely, you will discover the steps he or she followed before making that decision. A possible response to your question might be, "Well, first I looked at some ads, and then I talked to some members of my family who had recently bought cars, and then I went around to some dealers for test drives. Then I narrowed it down to two dealers, because they seemed trustworthy." If you listen carefully, you will hear the person's step-by-step decision process. The process may not differ much whether he or she is buying a car, hiring a new person, or buying what you have to sell, whether it's a product or an idea.

Influencing the Geller/Idealist

"...I have a dream that one day on the red hills of Georgia the sons of former slaves and the sons of former slave owners will be able to sit down together at the table of brotherhood. I have a dream that one day even the state of Mississippi, a desert state sweltering with the heat of injustice and oppression, will be transformed into an oasis of freedom and justice..." With these words the Reverend Martin Luther King, Jr., made history. He delivered them in his famous "I Have a Dream" speech at the Lincoln Memorial, on August 28, 1963, addressing a crowd of more than a quarter million people—and the media broadcast his dream to an audience of millions more.

With his use of metaphor and imagery, his emphasis on the future, his creation of a shared mission or common vision, and his stirring of the emotions, King was a model Geller. His speech survives as one of the finest examples of Gelling—the style of the idealist—in action. People who use this style effectively mobilize the energy and resources of others through appeals to their hopes, values, and highest aspirations and dreams. They strike a common chord, as King did, and inspire us to help support them in achieving their goals. They know how to convince us that their goals are *our* goals.

Gelling and the Entrepreneurial Vision

Of course, while Gelling is a very powerful style of influence, it is not always well received in the business environment, where rationality and logic are the prevalent modes and where short-term thinking often short circuits any idealism. But these days, especially in entrepreneurial companies, the visionary is being seen as a valuable contributor. As with the other styles, you of course must be aware when it is appropriate to use this style. If you were trying to influence someone whose preferred style is Felling, the use of imagery, metaphor, and poetic symbols would only cause the Feller to become suspicious, call the ideas "blue sky," or label you unrealistic, a dreamer, or a flake.

Creating a Sense of Shared Mission

The magical thing about the Gelling style, when it is used appropriately, is that people who use it kindle excitement about a better future, a future which other people value. Focusing on desired outcomes and goals—the future—can often be much more effective than focusing on current problems. This is not to say that problems should be ignored or shoved under the rug. But sometimes getting people excited about their own goals and dreams can actually move you more quickly to solutions of current problems.

In any influence situation, if you have the attitude that you are trying to support the other person and help him to achieve his goals as well as your own, you will be a most effective influencer. Your goals may *seem* different, but the person who uses Gelling skillfully will find a way to join her goals to those of the other, so that there is a true sense of shared mission or purpose.

When can the Gelling style be most effective? Usually, when you need commitment from several different people or groups, and also when individual values and interests must be joined for a larger goal or project.

The Geller Unpersuaded

Conversely, Gelling would be ineffective when trust has not yet been established or when rapport has not been achieved. In addition, this style doesn't work well when a quick solution is needed. Gelling takes time. It requires developing relationships, gaining trust, and slowly joining values and resources for a shared mission.

The Most Commonly Asked Questions about the Six Styles

To round out this chapter, let's take a look at some of the questions I get in my workshops about the six influence styles.

Question. Can a person really change his or her style of influence or is it an inherent part of a person's character?

Answer. Most of our behavior is learned. The style or strategy of influence which you currently use is also learned. There is no reason you can't learn additional strategies of influence. This learning is designed to increase the choices you have when you find yourself in a situation that requires influencing skills. In the next chapter, we will practice the skills necessary to master each of the six styles of influence.

Question. Is any one of the six styles better than the others?

Answer. No. Each style can be useful and effective in certain situations and with certain people. We'll look at some of these situations throughout the remainder of this book. The important thing is to know where and when different styles work and don't work. Attentiveness to the style of another person and the flexibility to alter your own style are the keys in influencing people effectively!

Question. What happens when you meet someone whose style does not fit into any of the six profiles? What do you do to influence this person?

Answer. Experiment until you find out what works. Look at the other person as a "ministudy." Collect data. The key is to be attentive to the other person and flexible enough to alter your strategy. To the extent that you can be aware of what you are doing and can change your strategy when appropriate, you will be effective.

Question. Do the six styles further subdivide or cluster?

Answer. Yes. The styles can be clustered, some overlapping.

- Telling, Compelling, and Felling form a cluster. All are logical, rational, and structured. Behaviors are proactive, controlling, and direct in their attempt to influence. These are often referred to as stereotypically masculine behaviors.

- Welling, Selling, and Gelling form another cluster. All are flexible, emotional, and receptive. Behaviors are less controlling. Listening behaviors are also found in each of these styles. These are often referred to as stereotypically feminine behaviors.

- Compelling and Selling form a third cluster. Compelling uses rewards (negotiations and bargaining) as a means to influence. Gelling offers benefits. However, there is an important distinction between these two styles. Compellers tell you what your rewards are. Sellers gather information on your needs and then try to match the reward with the need.

In order to reach your maximum potential as an influencer, you need to be aware of and adept at using all six styles as summarized in Table 11-1. Each style has its benefits and limitations. By using only one style

Table 11-1. Influence Styles

Characteristic	1. Telling/Analyst	2. Compelling/ Pragmatist	3. Felling/ Preservationist
Attempts to influence by	Reason, logic, evidence, data	Bargaining, negotiating, invoking higher authority, rewards, punishments	Winning over others, pointing out flaws
Values/likes	Structure; rational discussion of substantive issues	Give and take, dispensing rewards, outlining negative consequences	Brass tacks; status quo; short, direct factual discussion of current issues
Dislikes	Talk that is too emotional	Theoretical discussions; emotions, philosophy	Impractical, vague, fuzzy, ideas
Appears	Cool, studious, scientific	Knowledgeable, in control, hard to dispute	Judgmental, critical, able to grasp inconsistencies or contradictions
Apt to express	General rules, systems, structures	Noncomplex ideas, values of rewards	Rules, policies, sticking to a position
Apt to use	Long discussions, well-formed arguments	Case examples of past negotiations	Reasons, evidence of impracticality
Effective when	Problems are clearcut; precedents set	You have authority and power	Others look to you for "reality" test
Ineffective when	Creative solutions, new ideas needed; exploring uncharted areas	Long-term commitment to broad goals required	Ideas are new; "budding" stage
Strengths	Articulate, logical; sees rational issues	Comfortable with negotiation; can see both sides	Holds firm to a position; minimizes risks
Weaknesses	Difficult to change feelings with facts	May smooth over differences too quickly	May not gain long-term support or commitment

Table 11-1. Influence Styles (*Continued*)

Characteristic	4. Welling/ Catalyst	5. Selling/ Strategist	6. Gelling/ Idealist
Attempts to influence by	Listening, gaining rapport, joining	Presenting ideas in benefits; targeting to others' needs and goals	Creating and joining common visions, dreams
Values/likes	Personal relationships, self-disclosure, affective side	Challenge of understanding individual needs and decision strategies	Open exchange of ideas, dreams, goals, "big picture"
Dislikes	"Pure" facts, brief summaries, lack of emotion	Lack of information, curt, abrupt exhanges	Cool, rational discussion or analysis of data
Appears	Warm, supportive, flexible	Personable, open, knowledgeable, articulate	Attentive, perceptive, includes others
Apt to express	Empathy	Benefits, results	Future scenarios, emotions, metaphors
Apt to use	Different styles with different people, groups; personal anecdotes	Different strategies; slow "entry"	Indirect questions, ways to gain consensus
Effective when	Long-term involvement and commitment needed; solutions depend on close collaboration	Dealing with multiple stakeholders, constituencies, and issues; a "targeted" strategy required	Values and interests must be joined for larger goal or project
Ineffective when	Quick solutions needed; others lack initiative and expertise	Little personal contact and unable to send signals and cues	Trust not established, quick solutions needed
Strengths	Establishes trust; long-term relationship, commitment	Both prepared and flexible; astute listener for "cues"	Entertains novel, creative solutions; "blue skies"; delays quick fixes
Weaknesses	May seem to lack opinion or position	May change larger goal or position to get agreement	Can be distracted by emotions or dreams; delays decisions

you are operating at only one-sixth of your capacity (actually less than that). You need to recognize where different styles work and don't work and know how to alter your strategies accordingly. Choice is implicit here – provided you have all the necessary skills.

12

Influence Flexibility Lab: Exercises to Expand Your Influence Repertoire

Here are some simple practice exercises on the six influence styles to help you develop your skills so that you can see each style in its purest form and become more flexible in their use. In the influence flexibility lab exercises, you are asked to depart from your conventional or preferred way of influencing, as indicated by your score on the Influence Styles Inventory, and challenge yourself to try to influence in ways you've never tried before. This is like physical exercise in which you try to isolate and work new and different muscle groups. And as with physical exercise, you may find it uncomfortable at first.

It would greatly enrich your practice and learning if you could find someone who would help you by role-playing each situation and style. You might even want to involve a third person as an observer to watch and listen to you and your partner practice and experiment with each style.

Since these are face-to-face simulations, I am not providing work space in the book. The idea is to involve real people, not just work things out on paper. You might, however, like to jot down some notes at the end of each exercise as a reminder of what you think you did well, less well, and what you would do differently next time.

You are being given exact cases and information so that you can concentrate on the processes you are learning and not have to spend your time focusing on developing your own content or situation. Later on, as you become more practiced, it will be easier to apply them to specific real-life situations that you are experiencing and want to change.

Influence Exercise 19: Telling

The first style to practice is the Telling style. Specifically, you will observe Telling in its purest form and practice using the skills of this style. Keep in mind the characteristics associated with the Telling style of influence. Remember, the hallmark of the Telling style is the use of logic rather than emotion. People who use the Telling style use reasons and evidence to build their argument or case. They are fond of structure and are highly organized, and even when they appear to be integrating their ideas and their points with others, they usually do so in a structured and often meticulous way.

In Exercise 19, it is important that you use *only* the skills associated with Telling. Try to avoid using any other style. This effort may feel awkward, even when you're writing things down and planning, but it is important to observe and practice each style in its purest form so you will be able to recognize it when others are using it. Of course, in reality you should not use only one style. The real skill in influencing comes in orchestrating combinations of styles. Remember, you will be trying to read the other person; you therefore need to be attentive to his or her preferred style and flexible enough to adapt your style to his or hers. But before you can do this, you must become adept at recognizing and practicing each style in its purest form.

When can the Telling style be most effective? When the problems are clear-cut and there is a right-or-wrong, black-or-white kind of situation. It can also be effective when precedents are already set, that is, when there is already a format, policy, or procedure for this situation. When you are the only readily available source of information on the topic and when you are being looked to as the "expert," the Telling style is certainly appropriate. Another situation in which this style can be effective is when you are trying to influence another person whose own style of influence or communication is one of logic, facts, and reason.

When is it *not* effective or appropriate to use the Telling style? When creative solutions or new ideas are needed, or when you are breaking new ground, the pure explanation or reasoned evidence style may not work too well or impress the other person. Furthermore, when there are feelings involved, you will find that it is difficult to change feelings with pure facts. Later, you'll discover the most important variable in any influence situation—the seventh secret—which shows you how to use the influence style of the other person.

Influence Exercise 19: Telling

The first exercise is a simple one to help you learn the specific and unique characteristics and behaviors associated with Telling. You will be given a practice case. Since you're practicing the Telling style, remember to use only the strategies employed in Telling, namely, logic, reason, factual evidence, hard data, details.

DIRECTIONS

1. Try to influence someone (you may have a particular person in mind, if not, be creative and pretend) to do something which would be beneficial to his or her health.
2. Use all the logic, reason, and factual evidence you can muster.
3. Since the other person may resist, try to anticipate the specific points of resistance. Plot in advance, using reason and logical arguments, how you will handle their "yes, buts."
4. If you anticipate that you will get some resistance from the other person (suppose they say that they are too tired to exercise), then you can counter with the fact that exercise *reduces* chronic fatigue. Write out your initial argument, and then write the "objections" or "yes, buts." Be sure to use only the skills of the Telling style.
5. When you are done, ask yourself what difficulties you experienced. If your primary style is one of the others, you may have found it difficult and unnatural to think in such a logical, structured way when trying to influence someone. A little review will help you.

SCENARIOS

Since this is your first practice exercise using the styles, here are some scenarios you might want to try.

Scenario 1. You may want to persuade your spouse to improve his or her diet by avoiding high-cholesterol foods. Here are some hard facts that you can use to convince them:

- National Institute of Health reports that lowering elevated blood cholesterol levels will reduce the risk of heart attack caused by coronary heart disease.

- According to the American Heart Association, more than 50 percent of American adults have cholesterol levels above 200, a level at which the risk of heart disease begins to rise sharply.

- You need to broil, bake, steam, or boil foods instead of frying them.

(Continued)

- You need to eat foods with lower cholesterol level—fish, chicken, ½ percent milk, polyunsaturated fats—fresh fruits and vegetables.

Scenario 2. You may want to persuade the other person to stop smoking. Here is some evidence to back up this idea:

- The American Cancer Society estimates that cigarette smoking is responsible for 85 percent of lung cancer cases among men and 75 percent among women—about 83 percent overall.
- The cancer death rate for male cigarette smokers is more than double that of nonsmokers, and the rate of female smokers is 5 percent higher than for nonsmokers.
- Smoking is related to 320,000 deaths each year and costs the nation more than $27 billion in medical care.
- Remember that besides tar and nicotine, cigarette smoke contains a host of other poisonous gases such as hydrogen cyanide, volatile aromatic hydrocarbons—especially carbon monoxide—possible critical factor in coronary heart disease and fetal growth retardation.
- Death rates of cigarette smokers from coronary heart disease are at least double of those of nonsmokers.
- Cigarette smokers have 70 percent more heart attacks than nonsmokers.
- Smokers suffer 65 percent more colds than nonsmokers.

Scenario 3. Try is to convince someone to start to exercise. Here is some useful data on which your arguments can be based:

- Being unfit causes 85 percent of back problems and many joint problems.
- Exercise improves blood circulation throughout the body.
- Exercise helps an individual handle stress—so that you can do more.
- Exercise increases your strength, endurance, and coordination.
- Exercise reduces chronic fatigue.
- Exercise can help you lose weight.
- Exercise delays the aging process.

Influence Exercise 20: Compelling

If you are inclined to be a Compeller, you may find this exercise easy to do. You may use scenario 3 — the health and fitness arguments and facts — from Exercise 19 on Telling, or you may use another situation of your own choosing.

For now, to practice the Compelling style:

1. Try to influence someone to do or try something he or she hasn't done before.

2. Use bargaining or negotiation. Offer rewards if you get a "yes" response and possible negative consequences if you get a "no" response.

3. If you use scenario 1 (the improve-your-diet scenario) from the Telling exercise, you can use some of the statements that cite important or respected organizations or authorities; for example, according to the American Heart Association, more than 50 percent of American adults have cholesterol levels above 200, a level at which the risk of heart disease begins to rise sharply.

4. You may find it helpful first to write your argument and then to indicate the possible objections, or "yes, buts," the other person might come up with. And then you may want to add how you would overcome possible negative responses in order to exert your influence and get the result you want.

5. Finally, when you are finished with this exercise, reflect on the difficulties, if any, you experienced. If you think you're not a Compeller, you may have found it difficult to use this style in its pure form.

6. How did it feel to use Compelling as a style to influence another person?

Influence Exercise 20: Compelling

Now let's practice the skills and behaviors of the Compelling style in its purest form. While it may seem arbitrary and unnatural to use only a limited range of arguments or behaviors, remember that you're doing a practice drill, keeping each style in its purest form so you can learn how to use it. Keep in mind the behaviors and characteristics associated with the Compelling style of influence. Remember that Compelling is characterized by the use of bargaining and negotiation. People who use this style often offer rewards for complying with their proposals. They let you know their goals and expectations. Often they bring in a higher authority and sometimes they name-drop to let you know they have the ear or respect of the boss or someone else of high status or power. They also let you know the negative consequences you may incur by not complying with their wishes or requests.

As you should understand by now, the Compelling style usually works best when you already have some power or authority. Since you have to offer rewards or dole out negative consequences or punishments, it has to be assumed that you have something to offer the other person. And of course, it is helpful when the other person's level of motivation or their need for the rewards you control is very high. This is the case, for example, if you're their boss or supervisor and they are dependent on you for keeping their job.

When can Compelling be ineffective? Usually, this style doesn't work very well when you need a long-term commitment to broad goals. It is also difficult to use this style when you are very far removed from the person you're attempting to influence, since there has to be a constant and visible reminder of the rewards or punishments. How did using this style compare with using the Telling style?

If you are able to get a partner to practice these styles, you need to get specific feedback on your performance. Ask the person what it was like when you tried to influence him or her using logic, reason, evidence, arguments. Or, you can ask yourself if you can easily detect what style a person is using, and then check with him or her to see if your guess was correct.

Influence Exercise 21: Felling

If you work in a large or bureaucratic organization or if you have had any dealings with government or state agencies, you probably have been on the receiving end of the Felling style. Felling is characterized by pointing out flaws or inconsistencies in the ideas or proposals of others; challenging these ideas as "unworkable" by, say, countering them with a statement like "It will never fly here." People who use the Felling style also want to maintain the status quo. Remember that Felling is the style of the *Preservationist*, of people bent on preserving or maintaining the present order of things. Fellers hold firm to their positions and are often seen as rigid or uncompromising. To practice the Felling style, do Exercise 21.

Influence Exercise 21: Felling

DIRECTIONS

1. Try to influence someone by pointing out the flaws or inconsistencies in an argument he or she has presented to you. Perhaps someone you know has just suggested or presented an idea that you think is crazy, impractical, or "blue sky."

2. Now, write a few negative statements about the impracticality or illogic of the idea or suggestion. If you want to use the scenarios from the Telling exercise (Exercise 19), you'll find corresponding counter-arguments in the scenarios below.

3. Hold firm to your position, using reason, logic, and evidence. If you are able to find a partner to work with, then your partner can be the person with the idea, and you can be the Feller who is trying to cut down the idea by presenting reasons it's bad.

For example, if the other person is trying to influence you to begin to do more exercise, you can say simply that you don't like to exercise. Reason enough, right? Or you could cite an authority. For example, "According to Dr. Henry A. Solomon, author of *The Exercise Myth*, exercise may pose a health hazard because the exerciser runs a risk of experiencing an acute heart problem during exercise."

4. After you have finished working on Felling, take a moment to think about the difficulties you experienced when using this style. If you are not inclined to be a Feller, you probably found it difficult or unnatural to rebut or cut down someone's ideas.

SCENARIOS

Scenario 1. Five good reasons not to change my diet

- My job requires that I eat in restaurants frequently.
- I don't like fish or chicken.
- I don't have time to prepare the food.
- It is more expensive to buy fresh fruit, vegetables, lean meat, and safflower oil.
- I like what I eat now.

Scenario 2. Five good reasons not to quit smoking

- If I quit smoking, I will gain weight. (One third of exsmokers gain weight.)
- I enjoy smoking.

(*Continued*)

- If I quit smoking, I'd be too nervous and miserable to be around. Smoking helps me relax.
- I've got to die sometime. I'd just as soon die happy with my cigarettes.
- It's too late. I've been smoking too long.

Scenario 3. Nine good reasons not to exercise

- I don't have time.
- I look ugly in shorts.
- I don't like to exercise.
- I can't stand pain.
- I hate sweat.
- I'll start next week, month, year...
- It costs too much money.
- According to Henry A. Solomon, MD, author of *The Exercise Myth*, exercise may pose a health hazard because the exerciser runs a risk of experiencing an acute heart problem during exercise.
- A poll taken at a recent New York City marathon showed that the divorce rate among participants was 340 percent above the national average.

As we discussed in the chapter on Felling, the positive characteristics of this style are that Fellers are often seen as the voice of sanity or as the "strainer of reality" when all about them are people coming up with "blue sky" or genuinely impractical ideas. The difficult part comes when this style is used too early in the process of idea exchange and development. Fellers often criticize or veto an idea when it is first presented. And new ideas, like baby chicks, are by their very nature wobbly and awkward. They need to be nurtured and seen positively early on, so that they can begin to develop and grow stronger.

When can Felling be most effective? As discussed earlier, while the Felling style has many drawbacks and limitations, it can also be very useful when others come to you for a "reality test" of a new or untried idea. I myself have someone that I bounce new ideas off before investing much time and money in them, because he's a Feller. He usually finds the most minute flaws in the scheme or helps me see where it could be shored up. Often, his comments are so sharp that by following his advice, I save time and money.

When is this style ineffective? When ideas are new, and you're exploring new ground, you need to sort them out in an atmosphere of *positive* appraisal, so that they can grow.

All of us, at one time or another, find ourselves on the receiving end of the Felling style. That is, you're the one presenting an idea or making a proposal, while others are pointing out flaws or inconsistencies in it. What do you do? First, it's important to realize that people who use this style are not out to get you personally. They have a great interest in taking an idea and testing it so that there are no conceptual mistakes. People who use this style are often perfectionists, and they don't like to make mistakes of any kind. They don't even like to see others make mistakes. They are not risk-takers—they don't like exploring the unknown on the chance that something useful might turn up. So, usually, when an unfamiliar or untried idea is presented to them, it can threaten their sense of order, certainty, and predictability. And they enjoy finding the one thing wrong with something—finding it gives them great satisfaction.

A Special Tip for Getting the Most Out of the Felling Style

It's possible to leverage the Felling style to your advantage. When I give an idea or a proposal to a Feller, I give it to the person in an early version, or a first draft. This gives them the opportunity to test it and offer suggestions and criticisms. By getting them involved early, I don't wait until the idea is thoroughly worked out and it is too late to change. I often actively *ask* a Feller for a critique or criticism. I don't present the ideas as something "new," "innovative," "revolutionary," or the like. That often is perceived as too threatening, too radical. I try to show how what I am suggesting is not so different from what has already been happening; rather, it's a continuation of it, just further along the continuum. I use words that are comforting to a Feller's preservationist mindset, such as *tradition, maintain,* or *preserve our position in the marketplace.* As a part of this exercise, try reversing roles and putting yourself on the *receiving* end of the Feller style.

The following story about Sam, an aspiring marketing executive, illustrates how a Feller's input can be extremely valuable, and how, when confronting a Feller, attentiveness and flexibility can lead to a win-win outcome for all concerned.

Influence Scenario 5

Getting to Win-Win No Matter Where You Start

Sam had started work in the marketing department of a major toy company a month ago. His department's latest assignment was to develop a marketing plan for a new talking doll. Sam wrote a prospective marketing plan and distributed it to his coworkers to build support before the brainstorming session with the marketing vice president and the product manager. A day before he met with them, he went to see his supervisor about the proposal.

His supervisor read Sam's proposal, shaking his head all the way through it. After he finished reading the proposal, he said, "It's an interesting approach, but it's not the way we do things here. I don't think you ought to bring it up." Sam's first response could have been passive. After all, he was the new kid on the block, and his self-confidence wasn't at its highest level. He could have decided to take his supervisor's opinion at face value and wait for another opportunity to make his mark. But instead of becoming increasingly disappointed as his supervisor read the proposal, Sam just watched and listened.

As his supervisor listed his minor objections, Sam recognized he was in a Felling situation. The problem was that the proposal was new and different, not that it wouldn't work. And Sam knew he had the support of his coworkers. So, instead of being acquiescent and taking the negative message at face value, Sam decided to use the "no" as a starting point to discover the real issues. After a few probing questions about the proposal, Sam discovered that his supervisor's real opposition wasn't to the proposal as such, but to Sam himself. His supervisor simply didn't want to have his authority eroded by a newcomer.

Sam listened to his supervisor's minor disagreements with the proposal and the two of them worked out a compromise. His supervisor, representing the entire department, would make the presentation, and Sam would receive credit as the originator. The supervisor maintained his authority, and Sam got recognition.

This turned out to be a win-win situation for Sam, his supervisor, and the company. But the win-win opportunity was there only because Sam listened, observed, and was equipped to influence the situation. He didn't accept his supervisor's negative message at face value. Observation, by the way, is also part of listening. You have to "listen" to how a person presents the information nonverbally. *How* a message is communicated is as important as the message itself. (More on this in Part 3.)

Influence Exercise 22: Welling

Now to practice the Welling style. It's the style of the *Catalyst*. People who use it are often seen as the catalysts for other people's ideas – they are the power behind the throne, though they don't usually see themselves as powerful.

Influence Exercise 22: Welling

You can do the Welling practice exercise on your own by writing your influence strategy, or you can practice with a friend or colleague and give each other feedback. Here are your instructions:
1. Present an idea to someone.
2. Acknowledge that there are some areas where you lack expertise, and ask for theirs. Remember to ask for input and suggestions as you go along.
3. If you are hearing the other person's idea, you may offer suggestions only when they are asked for. When you are listening, make sure that you listen to what the other person is saying as purely and as clearly as you can, without interjecting your *own* ideas.
4. After you have worked out a Welling strategy on paper or have practiced the Welling style with someone, write down any difficulties you experienced with this style. For example, was it hard to listen to the other person without commenting or telling them how you might have done something differently? If so, why? How did it feel to use Welling as a style to influence another person?

If you are already inclined to be a Weller, you may have found it relatively easy to use this method. If not, you may have felt awkward or found it a strain to do the pure listening and the self-disclosing, both essential aspects of this style.

Let's quickly revisit some of the characteristics of the Welling style. Wellers are excellent listeners. They practice active listening, tuning in to other people. They are excellent at gaining rapport with others — it seems to be quite natural. They are often quite open in disclosing themselves to others, uninhibited about revealing their human frailties and imperfections. While others are reluctant to do this, for fear it will seem weak, Wellers know that this can be a very important way to bond and make a connection with others. Wellers are also extremely flexible, and they are quite willing to change the *form* of their ideas or presentations to that of the other person. Earlier, I mentioned that attentiveness and flexibility are the main keys to influencing. Wellers seem to practice them naturally — they practice attentiveness by tuning in to the content and the process of the other person's communication, and then they are flexible in shaping their own communication.

When can Welling be most effective? Usually, when you need long-term involvement and commitment from the other person, and also when solutions depend on close collaboration with one or more people. Of course, it can be extremely helpful when you are trying to influence a person who has important knowledge and skills you lack, in which case it is in your best interest simply to listen, and appreciate the gift you are getting of that person's wisdom, advice, and expertise. When another person is defensive or highly resistant to being controlled or persuaded (such as someone who has a natural suspicion of salespeople or of anyone trying to convince him of something), the Welling style can be disarming.

When is Welling most ineffective? When you need a quick solution, there might not be time to canvass everyone's opinion and listen patiently to every idea. Or, when other people lack the confidence, initiative, and expertise that is needed, using this style as a catalyst often won't produce a solution.

Because the Welling style differs from the other influence styles in its complexity, its principles really form the basis for the key to the secrets of influence. That is, to really influence effectively, you must be constantly attentive to both the style *and* substance of the other person; then, you must be flexible enough to adapt your style to mirror the other's. You must learn all the different ways one can be attentive and truly listen.

To deal effectively with Wellers, keep the following in mind:

- Establish trust. Begin by building a personal relationship.
- Draw them out. Ask questions about their thoughts, ideas, philosophies.
- Allow them to get to know you, not just as a business colleague, but as a person. Share some personal information; it need not be your deepest secrets, just a detail or two that sheds light on the human side of you.
- Let them in on the process of what you're doing. Don't present ideas as finished, but as taking shape and needing their contribution.
- Show yourself as being warm and supportive.
- With Wellers, it's okay to talk about personal feelings; they value feelings as much as facts.

Try to practice Welling with a Weller. Try to influence one, and you'll see how responsive they are to the style with the human touch.

Influence Exercise 23: Selling

Exercise 23 gives you practice incorporating several of the skills of the Selling style and getting hands-on preparation for a real-life Selling sit-

Influence Exercise 23: Selling

1. Goal/outcome (What do I want?):

   a. Ultimate Goal:_____

   _____

   _____

   _____

   b. Subgoals, or milestones:_____

   _____

   _____

   _____

2. Person (who has the power or authority to say "yes")?

   _____

   _____

3. Features/benefits:_____

   _____

   _____

   _____

   a. What are all the benefits that can be derived from the

   features?_____

   _____

   _____

   _____

   _____

   _____

   _____

   _____

(Continued)

b. Which specific benefits might appeal to this person?

_____

_____

_____

_____

4. Objections ("yes, buts"):

   a. What objections can be anticipated?_____

_____

_____

_____

_____

   b. How will you overcome them by presenting value that outweighs the objections?_____

_____

_____

_____

_____

5. Person's decision-making process:

   a. Examines all options:_____

_____

   b. Consults experts or a third party:_____

_____

   c. Makes quick decisions:_____

_____

   d. Makes tentative choice, then changes:_____

_____

   e. Other (please specify):_____

_____

uation you may be facing right now. The Selling exercise gives you space to write some notes about a current situation.

In responding to question 1 about your goal or outcome, make sure that you are clear and specific about what you're going to be asking for. For question 2, provide the "who." Write key points about the person you're trying to influence. For question 3 on benefits, record the specific benefits to the other person of your offer. In question 4, try to anticipate the objections, the "yes, buts" the person might give you, and write down how you can create value to outweigh them. You can refer to the list presented on page 107, "Barriers to Ideas—Roadblocks," to see how you might overcome each of the possible objections you might encounter. Imagine that you have enough information about the situation, and try to outweigh the negatives by building value or handling the objections.

In question 5, think about the prospect's decision-making process and outline it on paper. Also note what his or her underlying motivation might be.

Finally, when trying out Selling, keep in mind that this influence style is distinguished by its eclectic nature. In other words, it employs techniques from the other styles whenever the situation calls for them.

Influence Exercises 24–25:
Gelling

Let's review some characteristics of the Gelling style that you can use when doing Exercises 24 and 25. People who use the Gelling style can effectively mobilize the energy and resources of others. Gellers appeal to the hopes, values, and highest aspirations and dreams of other people. Gellers strike a common chord to gain support and achieve goals.

For Exercise 24, choose a current situation in which you would like to influence and inspire a person or a group. Write some notes and then a few sentences that express your idea in terms of the language of the Gelling style—using emotional words, strong imagery, and metaphor. Then, try to zero in on what the goals and missions of the persons you're trying to influence might be, and see how you can build bridges to join your mission with those of the person you've targeted.

In the workspace provided in Exercise 24, there are questions for you to ask someone when you want to practice the Gelling style. The "Present State—Desired State," questions give you a process to use to help people discover their current situation, what their desired or ideal situation is, and how they would know when they achieved it. Using

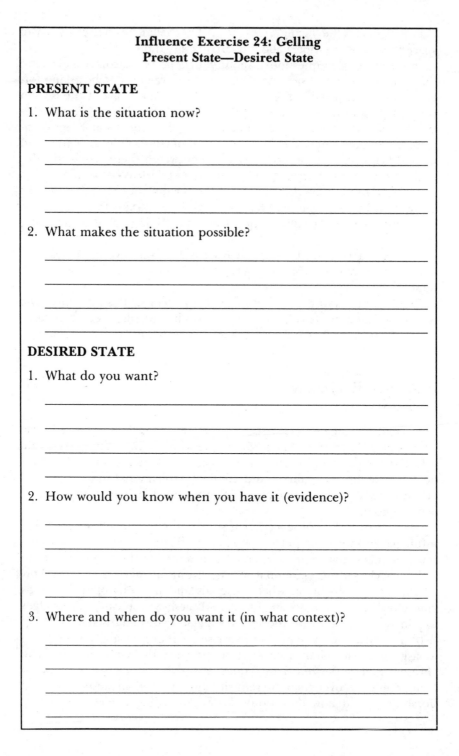

Influence Exercise 24: Gelling
Present State—Desired State

PRESENT STATE

1. What is the situation now?

_____

_____

_____

_____

2. What makes the situation possible?

_____

_____

_____

_____

DESIRED STATE

1. What do you want?

_____

_____

_____

_____

2. How would you know when you have it (evidence)?

_____

_____

_____

_____

3. Where and when do you want it (in what context)?

_____

_____

_____

_____

4. What stops you?

_____

_____

_____

_____

5. How will having it change or improve conditions?

_____

_____

_____

_____

6. What resources would you need to get it?

_____

_____

_____

_____

7. What strategies or paths could you use?

_____

_____

_____

_____

these questions can be a very powerful way to establish rapport and truly align yourself with another's goals.

If used appropriately, the Gelling style can kindle excitement for a better future, a future another person values. Knowing what a person values, of course, is all part of gaining rapport. Thinking about people's present state versus their desired state is one way to help people discover their goals, and for you to discover their values at the same time. The group of questions called "Present State–Desired State" are effective to use when you encounter a situation that requires a vision.

Exercise 25 provides another process with two sets of questions to ask people. You ask them the first set of "problem orientation" questions and then write down their answers. Then, when you ask the second set of "outcome orientation" questions, you may see a dramatic shift in their facial expressions, voice tones, and energy levels.

People are usually very down and have low energy when you ask questions about problems ("What's wrong?"), limits, and so on. These questions focus their attention on immediate problems rather than long-term solutions. When you change the frame, so to speak, to focus on desired outcomes, you usually create an accompanying shift to optimism and thinking about possibilities. This, too, is a powerful technique for Gelling.

Influence Exercise 25: Gelling
Problem Frame—Outcome Frame

PROBLEM ORIENTATION	OUTCOME ORIENTATION
1. What is your problem?	1. What is your desired outcome?
2. What's wrong?	2. What do you want?
3. Why?	3. How?
4. How are you limited?	4. What is possible for you?
5. What mistakes have you made?	5. How can you use what happened?
6. What did you do wrong?	6. What did you do right?

Notes—problem orientation questions:_____

_____

_____

_____

_____

_____

_____

_____

_____

_____

Notes—outcome orientation questions_____

_____

_____

_____

_____

_____

_____

_____

_____

_____

_____

PART 3

The Seventh
Secret
and Beyond

By now, you know how to determine where you and other people are in the constellation of influence styles, and you've learned some of the basics for turning this knowledge into greater influence. But there are a few more critical steps necessary to maximize your influence potential. In Part 3 of *The 7 Secrets of Influence*, you'll work on developing higher-level influence skills. Specifically, you'll concentrate on cultivating the kind of attentiveness and flexibility that bring people out and makes them more comfortable, more communicative, and more receptive to your ideas. You'll also learn about some shortcuts to establishing and maintaining a confidence-building rapport that will get you much more immediate and significant results.

13

The Seventh Secret: A Formula for Success

As you learned in Part 2, six of the seven secrets of influence correspond to the six influence styles. The secrets, of course, aren't the styles themselves. The secrets are knowing how to recognize the styles and how to use your knowledge of each style to your advantage when trying to exert your influence. In this chapter, you will discover the *seventh* secret of influence, the key skill for optimizing your influence.

When to Go with the Flow

The seventh secret of influence isn't another style. It's a formula. It expresses the most important principle in this book. In fact, this formula reveals the key to the successful use of all six styles:

Influence = Attentiveness + Flexibility

In other words, the amount of influence you exercise is in direct proportion to how closely you pay attention and how flexible you are. Now to explain this a little more clearly. *Attentiveness* is the ability to read another person, situation, and underlying clues. It is a human sonar system—a sensitivity to both verbal and nonverbal communication. *Flexibility* is the ability to shift to an appropriate behavior, depending on how attentive you are to the verbal and nonverbal clues the other person is giving you.

Learning How Best to Apply
Intuitive Skills

The formula above is the foundation of more than just influence. These human skills—flexibility and attentiveness—and their application have their basis in the science of cybernetics. *Cybernetics* is the comparative study of natural systems and systems of mechanical control in order to better understand communication and control in both systems. The goal of cybernetics is to understand why natural systems are more *flexible* than the systems that humans are capable of building, and then to apply this knowledge to manmade systems. By the same token, one of the goals of studing influence is to discover why intuitive skills are often more efficient than learned ones, and how we can best use our learned skills.

In this way, the goals of influence and cybernetics are analogous. This point is raised because one of the laws of cybernetics states:

> A unit or a single organism that has the greatest flexibility or the widest range of responses is the unit or organism that has the highest probability of survival or success in the overall system.

Sound familiar? The analogy is that if you have a high level of flexibility, you will not run out of possibilities or behavior options in situations requiring influence. For instance, many of us make the mistake of using the same behavior over and over to get what we want, as when we speak progressively louder to someone who doesn't understand English or is hearing-impaired. In the context of influence styles, this means, for example, that Gellers tend to stay Gellers, digging in to their ingrained patterns, and even seeking out others like them. Flexibility means acting on the realization that if a particular behavior isn't working, it's time to try a different behavior. Instead of speaking louder, you might find someone who speaks the language, or get a foreign-language dictionary, or use sign language.

You can think of flexibility this way: If you notice that what you're doing is not giving you the results you want, don't continue those same behaviors harder or longer. Stop, and try another tack.

If you can sense important clues by being attentive and can interpret these clues as a signal to change your behavior, then you'll have a better chance of getting what you want. You have to learn to alter your strategies to the situation and the other person in order to have more influence. In other words, match your style to the other person's style. (This concept is discussed in more depth in Chapter 17, which shows you how to match styles.)

Like Likes Like

The best way to effect change is first to understand how someone is influenced — which means being attentive to the style of influence the other person is using. Your level of flexibility is seen in your ability to adapt your style to match the other person's style. Remember, people who depend exclusively on one influence style to influence others will most likely be swayed themselves when confronted with that same style. They will feel more comfortable and less defensive if you speak their language. The other person's "language" means literally the key words they use. These are the verbal clues you have to learn to recognize. In the chapters that covered each influence style, you were introduced to some of the the key words and phrases that are indicative of each of these styles.

Think back to the list of words you were asked to make in the first group of exercises in Chapter 1. Check Influence Exercise 1 and look at the words you wrote. What words that influence you did you list? What style is represented by the words you wrote?

Suppose, for example, that the key word you used was *trust*. That is, the key ingredient that caused you to be influenced was that you trusted the person. What style is closest to this? If you think it's the Welling style, you're correct. Now, that's how you reported you were influenced by another. Are you also a Weller?

Or you may have listed such words as *shared vision* or *brighter future* as being the key elements that influenced you. What style do these words represent? They seem to be expressions of the Gelling style. Some people may have reported that they said "yes" when they were on the receiving end of someone's influence attempt because there was a clear *benefit* stated. And that the benefit seemed to zero in on some need or goal that they, the recipient, had. What style would that be? It sounds like Selling.

Most people reveal that the style in which they are influenced is very similar to their own influence style. This fact just reinforces the point that people are usually influenced in the way they — consciously or unconsciously — influence others. Like likes like. It's a basic principle in all nature, as you'll see in the chapter on rapport.

Develop an Ability to Be Flexible

Developing an ability to be flexible is a key concept for effective influencing. Wellers understand it well. If what a Weller is doing isn't working, he or she will try other techniques to get the desired result.

If you constantly act (or react) in every situation using the same tactics, they may work for you some of the time, but you'll increase your odds for success if you have a wider scope of strategies to use. In other words, if what you're doing isn't working, don't do it harder or louder or stronger, do something else! Almost anything else will work better than what you're already doing. Think of yourself as an experimenter and the arena of personal relations as a great laboratory. At first, it will be a matter of trial and error, until you learn what techniques will work best in different situations and with different people. But as you practice, you'll soon find that flexibility comes more naturally to you.

Rats = Humans? Perhaps you've heard the story about the difference between rats and humans. When you put a rat in a maze and let him know there's cheese down one of the tunnels, he goes down the tunnel and gets the cheese. Now, if you remove the cheese from that tunnel, what does he do? He'll go down the same tunnel a few times and see there's no cheese. After a while, he'll stop going down that tunnel. He may then try going into another tunnel to look for the cheese. But humans? We tend to keep going down the same tunnel long after we've had overwhelming evidence there's no cheese there.

Most people don't bother practicing flexibility—either because they're too lazy or are afraid to fail. (Remember, Thomas Edison made 1999 tries before he found the winning solution for the electric light!) Keep in mind that flexibility is the key to influence. It is an important element, and one well worth practicing.

Word matches reinforce the point that people are usually influenced in the way that they—consciously or unconsciously—influence others. Be attentive to what someone is telling you, and be flexible enough to use this information. Influence = Attentiveness + Flexibility. The more attentive you are in recognizing another person's style, the more flexible you'll be in dealing with that person, no matter what style is exhibited.

The Welling Style—The Seventh Secret in Microcosm

Just as influence is a skill that can be learned—not strictly an innate ability—attentiveness and flexibility are also skills that can be learned. You may have already realized that the Welling style has attentiveness and flexibility as inherent capabilities. A Weller is an astute listener—"When presenting my ideas, I *actively* encourage the suggestions and ideas of others"—and so is attentive. A Weller also possesses the ability to change or alter his strategies—"My communication style can change radically depending on who I'm talking to"—which is the flexibility to get the desired results. Wellers have finely developed attentiveness and flexibility skills and have learned to use them intuitively.

Because these principles in the Welling style are the foundation of an effective influencer, let's briefly examine the Welling style in terms of the seventh secret. If you are a Weller, you'll see how to sharpen these skills. If you're not a Weller, you'll develop an ability intuitively to combine attentiveness and flexibility to form an effective influence tool to supplement your own style.

By definition, a well is a source of abundant supply. A Weller uses this style as a source of support or information for others. One of the most important characteristics of the Welling style is the ability to establish rapport. A Weller can gain rapport in a number of different ways, like disclosing his or her own feelings to others, being loyal, and keeping confidences. Wellers self-disclose either by sharing a piece of personal information or by acknowledging imperfection. They tend to let someone know when they lack expertise. It takes a confident person to admit a lack of knowledge. Wellers also prefer face-to-face meetings rather than impersonal memos. Wellers want elaboration and explanation, not just the bottom line.

One of the common traits of Wellers that clearly exhibits their attentiveness and flexibility skills is their ability to work with groups, especially groups of people who have divergent goals and needs. The AT&T manager whose group work was profiled previously in the chapter on Welling is a good example. He uses this style with many different people and groups. In each meeting, he demonstrates attentiveness by listening to and observing each participant's thoughts, needs, and hidden agendas. He then demonstrates flexibility in shaping his idea so it is in harmony with the others. It is also significant that he doesn't have a large investment in the ownership of the idea. He doesn't mind that others get the credit for what turns out to be a good solution, even though the nucleus of the idea was his all along.

Welling is obviously effective on an individual level too, especially if the other person has knowledge, skills, or resources that you don't have. As an effective Weller, you often are satisfied just to gather information, without imposing or pushing a particular idea. And Wellers in positions of authority understand well the power of tuning into others, and they know how to lead by listening. The Welling characteristics of attentiveness and flexibility also can be the solution when another person resists being controlled or being told what to do. Wellers are often the most successful in top management in companies, and in environments where groups of people with different goals must be pulled together to accomplish a specific mission. Senior executives are not always Wellers on their way up, but once they reach the top, they find Welling the most useful style.

14

The Art of Listening: The Underrated "Power" Tool

Your attitude toward listening is as important as the skill itself.

Why Listening Is So Hard

Listening sounds like such an easy thing to do. All that's required is keeping your mouth shut and your ears open. But *really* keeping our ears open seems to be a herculean task for many of us. Why?

Distractions. Part of the answer is that we are faced with a multitude of distractions — both internal and external. Externally, a car alarm may be ringing outside. Internally, we may be worrying about traffic congestion on the way home. Or we may distract ourselves by deciding that the person we're speaking to is boring or intimidating. Perhaps she has mannerisms that annoy us or an accent that distracts us from what she's saying. Maybe we think a person is poorly dressed or that the subject he is talking about is low on our priority list.

Lack of Training. Sometimes, we simply tune out. We seem to enter a mental black hole. The mind of an untrained listener often randomly voyages across a vast uncharted territory of thought while appearing to pay close attention, even to the point of adding such appropriate responses as "really," "yes?" and "uh-huh."

Filtering.   Sometimes our inability to listen — to hear what people are actually telling us — occurs because generally we perceive the world in ways that reflect our own needs. We unconsciously use a filter that permits only limited information to reach us directly, and we tend to screen out whatever is incompatible with our own picture.

Self-Absorption.   Another cause of poor listening skills is our preoccupation with our own agenda. While the other person is speaking we are busy planning what we want to say and mentally rehearsing our responses. In effect, we patiently wait — or tune out — then at the first opportunity, jump in and talk.

Developing new approaches toward listening — and practicing them — are the "power" tools of influence.

Listening without Judging

The Japanese symbol for the word "listen" is composed of the character for "ear" placed within the character for "gate." This pictograph makes sense. When we listen to someone, we are, in effect, passing through the other person's gate and entering his world. When we are really listening we are receiving the other person's attitudes in an open, nonjudgmental way. Being so open-minded can be risky because the speaker's point of view may challenge our own.

According to Carl Rogers, a noted therapist and founder of humanistic psychology, most of us find it extremely difficult to listen to another person in this open way. We're too afraid that we may be changed or influenced. It takes courage, as the late senator and linguist S. I. Hayakawa said, to "stand in another person's shoes." To listen well is to view the world from another person's vantage point.

As a result, many of us listen as though we were trial lawyers interrogating a witness. We listen for contradictions, irrelevancies, errors, and weaknesses.

To listen in a truly open, nonjudgmental way requires a lot of inner security. Most of us are afraid to listen in this way because we believe that we might be *changed*, that our beliefs may be altered or that we may lose our identity.

But all that's required to listen in this way is *acceptance*, not necessarily *agreement*. Even if you really hear another person out, you can always return to your own beliefs and opinions. But first, you must listen with an open mind.

Listening in an open way, however, does not mean accepting everything you hear. That would be naive—and bad for business. It simply means evaluating *after* you get all the information, not blocking it out so that you never actually hear what the other person has to say.

When people know you are listening critically or judgmentally, they assume an internal and external posture of defensiveness and work even harder to intensify their own position. Psychological rigor mortis sets in. If, however, someone senses through your verbal and nonverbal behavior that you are listening openly and acceptingly (what educator George Leonard calls "soft eyes" listening), that person will feel far less threatened by you and be much more open. Lines of defense drop; consequently, he or she will feel freer to explore other angles or options—and will be much more receptive to what *you* have to say.

By listening to another person openly, you convey a forceful message. You say: "I'm interested in you as a person, and I think what you have to say is important. I'm not trying to judge or evaluate you. I respect your thoughts, and even if I don't agree with them, I know that they are valid for you."

When you practice this sort of listening, you'll find your attitudes and behavior are contagious. If you listen actively and respectfully, chances are that you will be *listened to* respectfully when it's your turn to speak.

Developing a Genuine Interest in Others

Really listening to others requires an attitude of sincere interest and curiosity and *an honest desire to see things the way another person sees them.* In a way, it's adopting a posture of innocence and being open to the other person. It requires that you temporarily suspend judgment—that for the moment you ignore yourself and your attachment to your own ideas (something Wellers are very good at).

For instance, imagine that you're visiting another planet and the individual with whom you are speaking is an intelligent being you have discovered there. Simply gather information. What does the extraterrestrial look like, sound like? What does she talk about? Remember—don't evaluate what you perceive, and don't judge it, even to yourself as good, bad, stupid, smart, or silly. Just observe. Imagine that when you return you have to report every word, idea, thought, characteristic, and mannerism of that extraterrestrial whom you've discovered.

Once you've trained yourself to listen in this way, you'll see and hear things you would have overlooked before. You may find that people are more intriguing or interesting to you. Observe, listen to, and sense people just for the purpose of data gathering. Ignore your urge to decide whether you like them, whether they are like you, or whether they fit into your frame of reference. If you can suspend judgment, you're apt to discover a better sense of rapport with others.

Learning to Ask Good Questions

Sometimes even when you want to know more about another person, you may hesitate to ask questions because you don't want to, fearing that it seems nosy. Usually, however, the contrary is true. Most people feel complimented when they are asked questions—they are flattered that someone is expressing interest in them (Wellers intuitively understand this). Next time, don't hesitate, just start asking!

The first key to asking good questions is *tuning into your own curiosity*. What do *you* want to know about this person? Once you know *what* you want to ask, use the following tips to get clear, informative answers:

- *Ask open-ended questions:* A shy or reticent person may take the easy way out if your inquiries can be answered with a simple yes or no. For example, instead of "Did you regret making that decision?," ask "How did you feel about making that decision?"

- *Create cycles of learning:* Use some facet of the person's answer to your previous question as a springboard to your next question: "Can you tell me more about why you decided to launch your own company?"

- *Ask for more detail:* Most people speak in generalities. The way to get more interesting, "meaty" information from them is to ask for more detail: "What specifically do you wish you could have done differently?"

- *Avoid turn-off questions:* "How" or "what" questions are usually better received than "why" questions. People often feel defensive when asked to explain their motivations ("why" questions). Often they haven't thought through their reasons or they don't wish to disclose them.

When you ask people *how* they did something, your interest in the process by which they accomplished something is flattering to them. You will also sometimes get an interesting inside look at their modus operandi (m.o.)—their way of doing things—which can help you in influencing them.

Here are a few general questions that can help get people talking:

- "What's your understanding of this situation?"

- "What are your goals for this project? What outcome are you looking for?"

- "I'm wondering...I'm curious about..."
- "How did you arrive at that decision?" or "What were the most important criteria for you in making that decision?" (These questions offer you a glimpse of their decision-making strategies, which can be useful for evaluating their capabilities in a particular area.)
- "What caused you to...?" or "What motivated you to...?" (Here, you're looking for underlying reasons, motivations, and catalysts to people's decision making.)

Try It, You'll Like It

Here's an exercise: Next time you go to a party or social function with a lot of new faces, see how much you can find out about the people with whom you talk. With new acquaintances, you might pursue information about their jobs or about what they like to do on weekends. With old friends, see how much new information you can glean from them. Chances are that you'll find out interesting information from the new people, and once you really take the time to listen, you'll be surprised at what your old friends tell you about themselves that you didn't know.

If you can master the art of asking questions and listening with sincere interest, you can almost guarantee that you'll rarely be bored. You'll begin to find subtle gestures, speech rhythms, expressions, vocabulary, values, ideas, and experiences interesting. And you'll find that most people, when they are nurtured by a good listener, open up and reveal the most interesting aspects of themselves.

To learn to listen openly you must work on your internal attitude. While that sounds simple, it is not always easy. It takes practice and discipline. And you can't fake it—many people have equally good radar and can tell when you're feigning interest or pretending to listen when your thoughts are elsewhere.

Test your own radar by listening carefully to television interviewers. Notice how often the question has nothing to do with the conversation that preceded it. Interviewers who work this way are pretenders. They're not really listening; they are most likely reading their questions from a prepared list. Good interviewers are good listeners, and their questions grow naturally out of the conversation they are having with the person being interviewed.

Once you train yourself in this way, you'll find it well worth the effort in terms of what you discover about people and the kinds of relationships you can build. In the next chapter on refined listening, we'll discuss more specific things to look and listen for.

Developing the Art of Helping with Silence

Many people believe that just listening without injecting comments or advice seems too passive or compliant. Their philosophy is: influential managers aren't passive; they act. It is a curious and unfortunate aspect of our culture that we tend to think that any action is better than no action, and that just listening or absorbing means you're a wimp, a procrastinator, or a do-nothing.

Jack Gibb, an early figure of humanistic psychology, often says "help isn't always helpful." What he means is that, even with the best intentions, we are often too directive. We tell others what they should or shouldn't do or what worked for us. While we feel helpful, we may not help others to arrive at the best solution for them. Neither do we empower them to stand on their own two feet and come up with their own solutions. Advice and information are usually seen rightly as attempts to change a person. They serve as barriers to self-expression. Ultimately the advice is seldom taken and the information is discarded.

Suppose someone in your life — your boss, a colleague, your spouse, or a friend — is telling you about a difficult situation he or she is in. Your simple task is just to listen, *without* doing all the other, non–pure listening things we all do. For example, try not to jump in and tell them about a similar situation you encountered once and how you solved your problem. And try not to refer them to some sources where they can find advice or help (until you've first listened to what they have to say). All your recommendations might be useful and well-meaning in their place, but by adding and intervening, you are not simply "being there" for the other person. And often, when people are having troubles or difficulty, all they really want is someone simply to listen. Chances are, your troubled friend, colleague, or relative knows the solution or can figure it out. What he or she needs, though, is someone just to be there, like a mirror.

Giving your advice and solutions will interfere with other person's use of his or her own creative problem-solving abilities.

In helping to change people, Carl Rogers based his entire method on simply listening to them. In developing what has become known as "client-centered therapy," he influenced people by "merely" listening — and knowing when to ask the right questions. He did not practice the more active or directive kinds of persuasion, but still managed to induce people to make profound changes. By acting as a sounding board to enable people to explore their own thoughts, Rogers subtly led them to make the most of their own knowledge and skills. The lesson: Never underestimate the power of listening.

Developing a Desire to Accommodate

Why be accommodating when you're trying to get people to think or do things your way?

Accommodation can be a key factor in softening someone's resistance, and it is an important quality of Wellers. In a study of negotiations, it was found that the most successful bargaining sessions occurred when one of the parties offered a few concessions (accommodations) early in the game. By offering concessions, these people changed the environment and were able to get more of what they wanted in the long run.

What this means is that sometimes we have to give up "being right" in the ultimate service of "winning." If you argue or try to talk people out of their needs and wants, you may score a point here or there, but you will probably not gain much in the way of trust. Nor will you make much progress in building a strong long-term relationship.

This doesn't mean you should approach a negotiation as though you're giving up everything you want. What's important is an *attitude* of willingness to consider the other person's point of view and a willingness to make a few concessions if necessary. In this way you can best achieve your ultimate goals.

Influence Scenario 6

The Customer Is Always "Right"

Kathy, a marketing manager at IBM, uses the right approach. When a client calls her to complain that a machine isn't producing the results the sales rep said it would, Kathy listens carefully without getting defensive and strikes the attitude that the client is *right* (at least for that moment—and certainly the client believes he's right). Then, she shows concern and empathy with a few well-placed phrases, such as "I can certainly appreciate your frustration" or "I know how important it was to get that data completed this week."

Sometimes she calls on irate customers to show them that her company cares about the productivity of its clients. Often, she finds that by the time she gets there, they have cooled off. Sometimes just letting them talk about what ticked them off can defuse their anger. Kathy has found that in the long run her company maintains customers more successfully if she is accommodating. For her, this helps to ensure the loyalty of her company's clients.

Practice Makes Perfect

Now let's practice several different kinds of listening skills.

Open Listening

This exercise will enable you to improve your listening abilities. You can do this exercise with a partner, or do it the next time you are having a conversation. Simply practice listening; that is, apply yourself to hearing what you are being told—try to be "all ears." One way to check yourself to see whether you're really hearing what you're being told is to observe, as you are listening, where your mind is going and what you are thinking about. For example, you may be making judgments, telling yourself that the speaker really hasn't analyzed the situation properly. You will find, after a while, that you become much more attuned to the other person.

It can be very instructive just to listen to all the "noise" going on simultaneously in your mind. After a while, try to eliminate some of it by concentrating more on the other person, and then see what happens to the quality of your conversation.

Try to echo, in words, what the person is saying. Suppose your friend says to you, "My boss is really giving me a hard time today." You can restate this by responding, "Sounds like your boss is on your case for some reason." For this kind of listening, the simplest kind, you don't have to ask concerned questions, or come up with advice or solutions. You can mirror simply to check whether you "got" the communication the way the other person sent it.

Active Listening

Another kind of listening, which is a little more proactive, is called *active listening*. This type of listening requires that you be more engaged or actively involved. An active listener "restates" the content of what is being said. This means putting into your own words the meaning of what has just been said. For example, suppose a colleague says to you, "The caliber of people I have been getting is forcing me to be more direct and forceful in order to get the work done." One way of restating this would be, "It sounds like you need to be more authoritarian in the way you manage this group." What you are doing is paraphrasing, or rephrasing, the ideas expressed by the person's words. You must be careful, though, not to use their words to express *your* thoughts so that you change the essential meaning. Simply try to clarify the phrase or sentence, without changing the basic integrity of what has been said.

Reflecting Feelings

Another active listening technique is called *reflecting feelings*. This technique is similar to restating in that you attempt to mirror back what you hear. However, instead of restating the ideas, you try to reflect the feelings or emotion behind them. For example, if someone says to you, "My friends always ask me to do favors for them as though they think I have all the time in the world on my hands." If you were to reflect the feelings of this statement, you might say, "You sound angry about that." Here, you are listening for the tone expressed by the spoken words.

Caution: When reflecting feelings, you are, at best, only *guessing* at the feelings the person may be having. So, you may want to try a few different feeling statements, "You sound like you're feeling overwhelmed and frustrated." Then, the other person has the chance to let you know whether your sense of the emotion they have is actually the correct one.

Open-Ended Questioning

Another active listening technique involves using *open-ended questions*. These are the kinds of questions that do not easily lend themselves to simple "yes" or "no" answers. Usually they begin with *what, why,* or *how.* For example, "What do you think you can do about the person?" "How can our friends learn to be more sensitive to you?" Try answering those with a simple yes or no! Open-ended questions are a great way to get a person to open up and share with you.

Precision Listening

The last listening technique is called *precision listening*. Since most language is vague and imprecise, there is a lot of slippage between the words and the experience being related. Although sometimes it is appropriate to speak in broad terms (such as when you want other people to access their own experience), often fuzziness of language is caused by imprecise thinking or speaking.

Precision listening is an active listening technique that enables you to identify the true meaning behind large abstractions or concepts or fuzzy communication. All words are symbols we use to describe our inner "maps" of reality. Problems occur, for example, if I assume that your symbol carries the same meaning as mine. For example, the word "recess" can mean a break in the school day to a child, a kind of lighting fixture to an interior designer, and something very different to a judge and jury. The skills of precision you are going to practice are tools to help you get a sharp focus on what other people's words mean to *them*.

Block-Busting Questions

Block-busting questions offer a way to elicit more precise communication from another person. Vague and imprecise communication is considered low quality. Using precision will help you to upgrade the communication you get from others to high quality.

Here's a simple illustration: Take the statement, "Let's work out an agenda." If someone said this to you in a work context, what would it mean? You might understand this as a project and go back to your workspace, *thinking* you knew what the other person meant but not being sure. Then, you'd scratch your head and try to work out an agenda according to what you thought the person meant. But unless you checked it out, you could be way off base. What does *agenda* mean to that person? Does it mean the list of events, the speakers, a detailed, step-by-step plan for the meeting, or just an overall outline? What is meant by *work out*, and who is going to be responsible for it?

There are various ways to frame questions to get the other person to be more specific. You can ask, "What, specifically, do you mean by...?" Or, "Can you give me some more information?" Or, "I wonder if you could give me an example of an agenda that worked well at your last meeting?" Or, "What information would you like included in the agenda?" Usually people speak in generalities and they believe the listener knows clearly what they mean. Asking block-busting questions breaks through to the true meaning and gets you the more precise, more specific information you need.

Influence Exercise 26: Block-Busting Questions

In Exercise 26, you will see some phrases and sentences that are deliberately vague and imprecise. Write all the block-busting questions you might ask in order to get more detailed and specific meaning for each one. You can also work with a partner, taking turns with the statements and then asking each other your "precision" questions.

Influence Exercise 26: Block-Busting Questions

For each of the statements below, ask yourself (or a partner) block-busting questions until you get more specific meaning and understanding of the sentence. Write (a) the block-busting questions you used and (b) the expanded, fuller statements.

1. "Let's work out the agenda."

   a. Block-busting question:
   Ex. What specifically do you mean by *agenda*?
   _____

   b. Revised statement:
   Ex. The list of events for the meeting.
   _____

   a. Block-busting question:
   Ex. What events?
   _____

   b. Revised statement:
   Ex. The stress management workshops.
   _____

   a. Block-busting question:

   _____

   b. Revised statement:

   _____

2. "I want to get that out today."

   a. Block-busting question:

   _____

   b. Revised statement:

   _____

   a. Block-busting question:

   _____

   b. Revised Statement:

   _____

   a. Block-busting question:

   _____

b. Revised statement:

_____

3. "Training should cover most of the policy procedures."
    a. Block-busting question:

_____

    b. Revised statement:

_____

    a. Block-busting question:

_____

    b. Revised Statement:

_____

    a. Block-busting question:

_____

    b. Revised statement:

_____

4. "Higher visibility will get us the notice we want."
    a. Block-busting question:

_____

    b. Revised statement:

_____

    a. Block-busting question:

_____

    b. Revised Statement:

_____

    a. Block-busting question:

_____

    b. Revised statement:

_____

(Continued)

5. "If we control the negotiations, we can anticipate better results."

   a. Block-busting question:

   _____

   b. Revised statement:

   _____

   a. Block-busting question:

   _____

   b. Revised statement:

   _____

   a. Block-busting question:

   _____

   b. Revised statement:

   _____

6. "Education prepares one better for management."

   a. Block-busting question:

   _____

   b. Revised statement:

   _____

   a. Block-busting question:

   _____

   b. Revised statement:

   _____

   a. Block-busting question:

   _____

   b. Revised statement:

   _____

7. "Middle management makes the most relevant decisions."

   a. Block-busting question:

   _____

b. Revised statement:

_____

a. Block-busting question:

_____

b. Revised statement:

_____

a. Block-busting question:

_____

b. Revised statement:

_____

8. "Trainees give us helpful feedback."
   a. Block-busting question:

_____

   b. Revised statement:

_____

   a. Block-busting question:

_____

   b. Revised statement:

_____

   a. Block-busting question:

_____

   b. Revised statement:

_____

9. "Let's work through the presentation."
   a. Block-busting question:

_____

   b. Revised statement:

_____

(*Continued*)

a. Block-busting question:

_____

b. Revised statement:

_____

a. Block-busting question:

_____

b. Revised statement:

_____

10. "Let's generate some business."
   a. Block-busting question:

   _____

   b. Revised statement:

   _____

   a. Block-busting question:

   _____

   b. Revised statement:

   _____

   a. Block-busting question:

   _____

   b. Revised statement:

   _____

11. "My boss is hassling me."
   a. Block-busting question:

   _____

   b. Revised statement:

   _____

   a. Block-busting question:

   _____

    b. Revised statement:

_____

    a. Block-busting question:

_____

    b. Revised statement:

_____

12. "Let's maintain a technical image."
    a. Block-busting question:

_____

    b. Revised statement:

_____

    a. Block-busting question:

_____

    b. Revised statement:

_____

    a. Block-busting question:

_____

    b. Revised statement:

_____

13. "Let's negotiate the contract to cover all contingencies."
    a. Block-busting question:

_____

    b. Revised statement:

_____

    a. Block-busting question:

_____

    b. Revised statement:

_____

(Continued)

a. Block-busting question:

_____

b. Revised statement:

_____

14. "We need to plan for anticipated growth."

   a. Block-busting question:

_____

   b. Revised statement:

_____

   a. Block-busting question:

_____

   b. Revised statement:

_____

   a. Block-busting question:

_____

   b. Revised statement:

_____

15. "I want you to exemplify the professional image for our trainees."

   a. Block-busting question:

_____

   b. Revised statement:

_____

   a. Block-busting question:

_____

   b. Revised statement:

_____

   a. Block-busting question:

_____

(Continued)

b. Revised statement:

_____

16. "Our attendance is down."

    a. Block-busting question:

_____

    b. Revised statement:

_____

    a. Block-busting question:

_____

    b. Revised statement:

_____

17. "The quality of our programs seems to be improving."

    a. Block-busting question:

_____

    b. Revised statement:

_____

    a. Block-busting question:

_____

    b. Revised statement:

_____

Influence Exercise 27: Comparators

Exercise 27 involves a list of words called *comparators*. These are words and phrases used to compare one idea to another. Often, comparators are imprecise and unclear. For example, your boss may tell you to be "more productive." Well, what specifically does that mean? More productive than what? Than you were last year? Last month? More productive than your coworkers?

You can ask precision questions to get a clearer understanding of what the person means when she uses comparators. You may respond to these statements by asking, "How do *you measure* productivity?" or "More productive compared to what, or who?" If you ask these questions directly, and in a way that indicates that you are seeking a better, clearer understanding, you will not seem to be challenging or threatening to the other person.

Influence Exercise 27: Qualifying Comparators

The following statements are called *comparators*, which are often used when comparing one idea to another. To avoid possible misinterpretation and get more precise information, statements like these must be qualified. Working with a partner, try your hand at qualifying the statements below to get clearer communication. Here are a couple of examples to get you started:

Comparator: That's a better way to do it.
Qualifying question: On what basis do you consider it better?

Comparator: We've had very good profits this year.
Qualifying question: When you say "good," what are you comparing it to?

1. That's a better way to do it.

   a. Qualifier:_Ex. Better than what?_____

   b. Qualifier:_Ex. What do you mean by *better*?_____

   c. Qualifier:_____

2. We've had very good profits this year.

   a. Qualifier:_____

   b. Qualifier:_____

   c. Qualifier:_____

3. I have a better idea.

   a. Qualifier:_____

b. Qualifier:_____

c. Qualifier:_____

4. Corporate wants more productivity.

a. Qualifier:_____

b. Qualifier:_____

c. Qualifier:_____

5. Doing it this way requires less effort.

a. Qualifier:_____

b. Qualifier:_____

c. Qualifier:_____

6. We should set higher standards.

a. Qualifier:_____

b. Qualifier:_____

c. Qualifier:_____

Influence Exercise 28: Universals

Another category of imprecise statements you may hear are *universals*, statements that declare that something is absolutely true. The way you can tell when people are using a universal is when they use the words *always, never, all,* or *none.* This indicates a black-or-white mode of thinking that often leads to hasty generalizations. In order to practice precision, you can ask simple block-busting questions, such as "How do you know all _____ are lazy?" or simply "All?" Such questions challenge the notion that what is claimed is always and forever true. You might also ask, "Can you think of a time when this was not the case?" thereby challenging the other person to question his or her own absolute thinking.

This really simple technique has been very successful in business, where often there is very unclear and vague communication, both orally and in writing. If people took the time to ask a few simple clarifying questions, they would have a wealth of clear, high-quality information, and they would be equipped to be much more powerful listeners, and therefore, better influencers.

Influence Exercise 28: Qualifying Universal Statements

For each of the statements below, write a few precision questions that might get the person to state the point more specifically. Then, write a revised statement you would like to elicit as a result of your question.

1. Each supervisor is responsible for her entire department.

    a. Qualifier: Ex. The *entire* department? ?

    b. More accurate revision: Ex. All the supervisory and hourly staff.

2. All management is concerned with is profits.

    a. Qualifier: _____?

    b. More accurate revision:_____

    _____

3. Everyone here supports one another.

    a. Qualifier: _____?

    b. More accurate revision:_____

    _____

4. My supervisor never notices the extra work I do.

    a. Qualifier: _____?

    b. More accurate revision:_____

    _____

5. Nobody shows me any respect.

    a. Qualifier: _____?

    b. More accurate revision:_____

    _____

6. Everyone does the easiest thing.

    a. Qualifier: _____?

    b. More accurate revision:_____

    _____

7. No one can do my job but me.

   a. Qualifier: _____?

   b. More accurate revision:_____

   _____

8. My manager doesn't trust anyone.

   a. Qualifier: _____?

   b. More accurate revision:_____

   _____

9. I can tell you every response she'll make.

   a. Qualifier: _____?

   b. More accurate revision:_____

   _____

10. We can't ever get what we need from the support staff.

    a. Qualifier: _____?

    b. More accurate revision:_____

    _____

Influence Exercise 29: Effective Listening Techniques

After you've completed Exercises 26–28, you can review the most effective listening techniques by doing Exercise 29. We've listed each listening technique with space for you to write your impressions and experiences when you try out each technique.

Influence Exercise 29: Effective Listening Techniques

Open-ended questions:_____

_____

_____

(*Continued*)

_____

_____

_____

Mirroring_____

_____

_____

_____

_____

_____

Restating_____

_____

_____

_____

_____

Reflecting_____

_____

_____

_____

_____

Precision_____

_____

_____

_____

_____

_____

15

Refined Listening: Fine-Tuning Your Radar

Any successful salesperson knows that no matter how great the product, it's not going to sell unless the buyer has a need for it. That need may be real (Mark *needs* a new coat because his has holes in it), or it may be perceived (Mark *needs* a new coat because he thinks his is out of style). And, of course, the good salesperson doesn't wait for the buyer to recognize his or her own need. The skilled seller is alert to the subtle cues that signal a customer's true needs, and then uses the cues to demonstrate how a particular item addresses those needs. How does the seller discover the buyer's needs? Through careful listening.

For most of us there are really only two times when we listen extremely well. The first occurs when something truly interests us. Even then our ability to listen can be negatively affected, for example, if we're preoccupied with a problem. Second, we also listen well when we know we must. In these situations we generally need to get specific information—answers to questions such as "How do I get to the highway from here?" or "Doctor, what do the test results mean?"

In order to be skilled at influencing others, it's important to master the ability to listen effectively in a broad range of situations. Then you'll be able to tune in to others when it's important to you—and when it's important to them.Earlier we examined the importance of listening and we looked at listening styles. The next step is to explore the process of *refined listening*—listening on a more subtle level and focusing on the more elusive elements of communication.

There are three important parts of refined listening:

- The context
- The content
- The medium

The Context of the Communication: What's the Environment?

The context of a communication includes both the external and internal environment of the interaction.

The External Environment

The external environment, of course, is the physical setting where the communication takes place—your office, someone else's office, a neutral work environment like a conference room, or a social setting like a restaurant. Whenever a conversation takes place on one person's turf, that person has a decided advantage in negotiation. That's because he or she feels more comfortable in that environment. If you are on neutral territory, then all things being equal, you will interact on a more equal basis.

The Internal Environment

The internal environment is the *circumstance* of your communication with another person. What emotional or intellectual factors are affecting each of you? What is going on in your lives at that time? What is the emotional setting? Is the other person tense or relaxed, feeling secure or shaky, depressed or elated over, say, a recent promotion? What is your relationship with the person? Is he above or below you in the organizational hierarchy? Is this a one-time encounter or an ongoing relationship? Is he responding with his own authority or ideas, or is he being influenced by others or by company rules or policies?

Influence Scenario 7

Feelings Can Get in the Way

David came into Pam's office and began to tell her about his discontent with his current job responsibilities. He complained about having been asked to take on the department's budgeting. He doesn't like budgeting and isn't good at it. While Pam might ordinarily have been sympathetic toward David, the internal context affected her reaction: She's been taking some accounting courses at night and has been trying to assume some of the department's financial tasks in order to gain experience in this area.

For this reason, Pam felt not only envious that David has been asked to do this work and she hasn't, but also insulted that the boss thought he'd be more competent than she would be. Her own personal interest in the situation inhibited her from responding the way that David would have liked. Instead of empathizing with him, Pam succinctly explained that she was busy and would have to talk to him later.

The context—and Pam's response—would have been different had her encounter been with a friend from another company who was overwhelmed with different job responsibilities. She would have been more detached, more sympathetic, and less personally concerned with the outcome.

The Six Rs

In any given conversation, evaluate the internal context of the situation. It is easier with people whom you know well, but it can also be done with those whom you've only just met. There are six variables to consider. Together they form the six Rs:

1. The Relationship. Ask yourself: What is the nature of your relationship? Have you worked together before or are you strangers? Is it strictly business or do you also have a personal friendship?

To gauge a relationship, measure these two components: longevity and intensity. For longevity, consider not only how long you've already worked with (or interacted with) this person, but also how long you expect to work with him or her in the future. For example, you may have a short-term relationship with certain vendors but a long-term relationship with most coworkers.

To measure intensity, consider the depth of your relationship. Is it a superficial, nodding acquaintanceship? Or is it a close relationship in which you will be working together as a team or as part of a task force over a given period of time? All of these factors have a bearing on the relationship.

2. The Range. What is the range of the other person's authority or responsibility in your discussion and in the organization as a whole? What is the range of his or her network of contacts within and outside of the organization?

3. The Record. What is the other person's history of response to you? What does this person's record for accepting new ideas or proposals reveal? Begin with whatever background information you can gather, and then make your own evidence-based judgment.

4. The Reasons. It's important to be aware of each party's reasons for communicating. To understand a person's motivations you may have to do a bit of guesswork, especially if you're in a situation where you don't know the person well. And you may have to begin with some probing and questioning to uncover what his or her real reasons and motivations are.

Suppose you're talking to a coworker in personnel, and you are trying to find out who is scheduled to attend the same management seminar that you are. If you're a typical upwardly mobile executive in a large corporation, then *your* reasons go beyond mild curiosity. You're wondering if you'll be grouped with anyone who could be helpful to your career. If so, you may want to do some homework and find out a little more about this person before you go.

The information you gain from your colleague in personnel will depend on *his* reasons for communicating with you. Perhaps he's also seeking favor with the person who would be of interest to you and he doesn't want to give you an edge. He may, however, share the information because there's no need for it to be secret, or because he sees that your success will benefit him as well. If you know the person well, you may already understand his reasons and may anticipate his reaction. If you don't understand his thinking, you would want to open with a general question about the seminar and move carefully toward the special information you want. Meanwhile, you would have had a chance to make some initial observations in order to predict a likely reaction.

5. The Rules. Rules are the fences that we build around our possible actions. They are our limits or boundaries. Rules are often expressed in statements that contain words such as *should, shouldn't, must, mustn't, have to, can't, always*, and *never*. It's important to be aware of the rules that govern another person's behavior, whether they are actually valid or exist only in that person's head. If the rules a person adheres to are valid in fact, they may be related to company policy, precedent, professional norms, or ethics. (In this case, know the rules as well or learn them by asking questions.) If certain rules are valid to only one person, they are constraints that the person believes to exist.

It's not your job to judge these rules or the person who follows them. Your only task is to listen and to be aware that personal rules represent restrictions and boundaries for that person's behavior. Rules—like the other Rs we've outlined—constitute a very important aspect of context with which you should become familiar.

When trying to determine context, you often have to use your best judgment to form some early assumptions, and then test your hypotheses by asking questions and gathering more data about the person's expectations, concerns, and desired outcome once you begin communicating.

6. Resistance. Resistance is very common in both selling and influencing. If you're lucky, you get a foot-dragging response, but not an out-and-out no. A resistance statement, such as "I'm not sure yet," "We've never done this before," or "We don't have enough time (or money)," usually means that the person is asking for something from you. It could be more information about what you're proposing, reassurance that he is not making a mistake, or more rewards or benefits that will be gained from saying yes to you.

Most people who are unaccustomed to resistance or do not anticipate it tend to become intimidated and anxious. They let resistance stop their efforts instead of using it to proceed further. Others rigidly persist in repeating whatever they were saying and doing, but say and do it louder and with more effort. This, of course, usually intensifies the resistance. Still others who are fearful of "losing" become too accommodating. These people tend to make too many concessions, or they become petulant or overly demanding.

Carole Hyatt, an international sales consultant and author of the best-selling *The Woman's Selling Game*, points out that "no" is far better than "maybe" as a response. She notes that you can be kept in "maybe land" forever, but once you begin hearing the specific "no's" you can better target your persuasion efforts. "You've simply got to become desensitized to 'no' and *not* hear it as a signal to stop," says Hyatt. "It simply means that the prospect is still uncertain."

Effective influencers realize that resistance is a natural part of the influence process. In fact, they welcome it as an important and necessary step in the process. As million-dollar salesman and author Elmer Letterman said, "The sale begins when the customer says 'no.'" Only then does the salesperson have an idea of whether the prospect needs more selling, more information, and more convincing, that is, more influence.

A "no" response also should send you back to the material covered earlier in the book to help you plan your strategy. What operating style does this person have? What style should you use to influence him or her? The specific skills discussed earlier now come into play.

The Content of Your Communication

Content is the substance of the message—what the person is talking about. *It is made up of all the words, facts, and ideas in a communication.*

With a few straight-shooting people, the content of the message is all there is—they say exactly what they mean. You probably know one or two of these brutally honest people. Some even preface their remarks with "I'm going to level with you...," and what you get from them is a direct opinion on the matter you're discussing. (Not all who use that phrase are so honest. You should still consider the context and the medium to be sure there's no hidden agenda.)

Too often in business, however, we act as if content is all there is in our interactions with people. While content would appear to be the simplest aspect of refined listening, it can sometimes be the most deceptive because it alone does not usually convey the speaker's entire message.

Influence Scenario 8

Listening between the Lines

Suppose Sam's boss gives him an important project to finish while she is away on vacation. It is a project that must be completed before she returns, and it will affect the boss's own performance appraisal. The content of their discussion includes a description of the desired outcome of the project plus the exact steps Sam is to follow to achieve that result. The boss prefaces their conversation by saying, "I want you to listen carefully...," a patronizing comment she has never made before. As she talks, she tells Sam exactly how to do things he's done many times before. She even mentions that she'll be going over the material with her own supervisor when she returns.

From these verbal content clues, Sam begins to pick up the *context* of the *content*: His boss is not comfortable delegating this task to Sam since he has never before handled such a project from beginning to end. As a skilled listener, Sam has absorbed the content, but he has also discerned the unspoken message. Depending on their relationship, Sam may even choose to introduce the *context* into the *content* by asking her whether this project has particular importance.

By picking up these content clues, Sam can use this occasion as an opportunity to shine. First, he may allay his boss's fears, and while she's gone, he can concentrate his efforts to perform the best he can. If Sam makes his boss look good, then in all likelihood he can anticipate a healthy career—in part thanks to his refined listening skills.

Suppose, in a conversation with a coworker, your colleague tells you about a friend who quit his job to start his own business and the business is thriving. Listening to the content alone will not give you the whole picture. Depending on the *context*, the story's *content* will take on different meanings. If you'd been talking about your own new business idea, your colleague may have been using this story to encourage you to move ahead. If you discern from the context that he has been feeling dissatisfied with his job, his content may be his way of hinting to you about his own hopes for the future.

The Medium of Your Communication

The medium is the packaging of communication. It provides the richest area for refined listeners, for it is here that you often get the most valuable information. The late Marshall McLuhan, Canadian writer and director of the Center for Culture and Technology at the University of Toronto, crystallized this idea when he coined the phrase "The medium is the message." He claimed that the external packaging of a message has more impact than the message itself—that the medium itself influences us. In other words, *how* you are told something is as important as the message itself.

You know it yourself, whether you're talking about perfume, a music video, or a person, the presentation counts. Especially with people, how someone looks, speaks, and dresses bears directly on what aspects of that person's message you hear, see, and believe. On the most elementary level, we would stop to give directions to a well-dressed man or woman who approaches us on the street. Yet many of us would turn from an unkempt person who asked the same question. When it comes to business, a job candidate preparing for an interview with a New York accounting firm might wear a conservative three-piece suit while his friend could wear a sportier blue blazer to interview with a Los Angeles–based advertising agency.

The way a person handles herself is crucial in determining the message we ultimately receive. Albert Mahrabian, a well-known researcher in nonverbal communication, notes that about 80 percent of the impact of any spoken communication comes from body language or other nonverbal types of communication. The Nixon-Kennedy debates during the 1960 presidential campaign are a confirming example. People who listened on the radio or read the speeches in their newspapers favored Nixon. Those in the television audience favored Kennedy. The difference was attributed to the nonverbal communication or the presentation styles of the two men. Kennedy's style of communicating led more viewers to believe in what he was saying.

Making a Start in Refined Listening: Borrowing from the NLP Model

What specifics can you watch and listen for when evaluating the medium of a communication? Psychotherapist Richard Bandler and linguist John Grinder have developed a model of human communication they call neurolinguistic programming (NLP). They analyzed the processes of effective communicators and broke their actions into identifiable, observable parts.

Most of us are not trained to notice these small bits of behavior unless they produce large changes, and we often misinterpret the changes we do see — a clenched jaw or crossed arms for example. We ascribe meaning to what we see based on our own use of these gestures or our past experiences with others.

Bookstores are filled with books on body language. Most of them indicate that a clenched jaw signifies anger, crossing the arms is supposed to convey disinterest or boredom, and blushing means embarrassment. The danger in interpreting these signals is generalizing too much. A clenched jaw may not always mean anger. It may indicate stress or a jaw condition. Blushing may not indicate embarrassment. It may signal frustration or anger.

What you can begin doing is to train yourself to notice the kinds of physiological changes described below. But don't generalize. Keep your observations specific to each person you're interacting with. If there are five people at a meeting, you may see five different sets of encoded, nonverbal behavior. What may seem like the same nonverbal response in two people may signal something very different about each person's internal state. For now, just notice and observe. Do not try to interpret or attribute any meaning to what you see yet. Later, you'll find out how to use the information you gather.

Tuning In to What's Unspoken

Body language can even be *more* indicative of a person's true state than the spoken word. There are several categories of nonverbal, unconscious, physiological responses that people exhibit and that you can look for. Usually these are actions outside of a person's conscious awareness. Here are some of the most important and easily visible ones:

1. Body Posture and Gestures

These body signals include:

- Sudden straightness of the spine
- Position of the head
- Position of the feet on the floor
- Distribution of weight on hips and lower legs
- Hand movements and gestures

As an experiment, the next time you're having a conversation with someone you know well, note as many of these signals as you can. At different times you may see the person's weight shift, moving from one leg to the other. For this individual, this posturing may indicate a change of mood or internal state—though for another person, it may indicate something else. What is the message in these weight shifts? Do they correspond with an air of bravado? Fumbling?

Let's say you have a friend named George who stands with his weight on his left leg when he's feeling confident. You may know this because he stood that way in your office when he told you about a successful presentation he had just made. When he feels nervous or uncertain, however, he places his weight on his other leg. You know this because you observed him doing it while he told you about a meeting he dreaded having to attend.

Make a friend or colleague your research population of one. Watch nonverbal signals closely. The person may, for instance, signal a shift in her level of confidence even if her words do not communicate it: "We feel confident that this method will work," she says, suddenly straightening her back. You'll need to observe your subject closely several times when you know he or she is feeling highly confident or insecure in order to recognize the differences in body language. After you practice, it will be difficult for your subject to fool you, despite the words being spoken. You will have gathered indisputable evidence of what the person's body does outside of his or her conscious control or awareness. Similarly, you can discover when a person is feeling supportive, interested, bored, disagreeable, or in some other mood.

For now, just observe and watch all the different variables in someone's repertoire of body postures and gestures. It is critical that your observations be descriptive, not evaluative. Your initial mental or written note should be "left leg weight shift," not "George seems ner-vous." In time, you'll begin to associate a particular posture or gesture with its corresponding internal state. There are more subtle but also easily detectable changes that you'll pick up once you begin noticing them.

2. Skin Color Changes

If you watch carefully, you can begin to see different colorations in a person's face at different times. For example, note the contrast between nose color and the skin color of the forehead. Blushes, of course, are easy to spot, but a blush isn't always in the cheeks. There are different types of blushes. Watch for them:

- At the tip of the ears
- On the forehead
- At the jawline

   The blush may be rosy and soft, a purply pink all over the face, or blotchy red. Some people blush when they're embarrassed, some when they're angry, others when presented with a challenge, still others when they're sexually excited. Again, your purpose as a refined listener is not to assign judgment, but just to observe these changes in any given person.

3. Minute Muscle Changes

Small muscle changes are idiosyncratic. Like other physiological re-sponses, they vary widely from person to person. Watch for:

- Muscle tightness or slackness near the edges of the mouth
- Tightness or squinting around the eyes
- Tightness at the jaw line
- The formation of creases on the forehead or directly between the eyes

4. Lower Lip Changes

These are the most common of the small muscle changes. Sometimes when people are feeling pressured or uncomfortable, their lower lip tenses. That's where expressions like *tight-lipped* come from. Some people seem to be this way all the time, but upon closer observation, you'll see that their lips are tighter at some times than at others.

Of course, tightness is not the only kind of lip change. Others include:

- Fullness
- Movement
- Size
- Shape
- Color
- Wetness
- Dryness
- Trembling
- Texture (smooth or rough)

Influence Scenario 9

Read My Lips

Janet, a marketer for a large cosmetics firm, always lets her colleague Sonya know, nonverbally, when she's open to an idea. Sonya, an astute observer of body language, notices Janet's lower lip enlarging and sometimes reddening. When Janet is completely closed to any new suggestions, she purses or tightens her lips. Before she's even said anything, Sonya may remark, "You don't like this idea, do you?" Janet is amazed at Sonya's perceptiveness, though this supposedly uncanny insight is based on nothing more than the kind of simple observation that you too can practice.

5. Breathing Changes

Changes in breathing are an early barometer of someone's mood. The easiest way to observe a person's breathing rate is to watch the up-and-down movement of their chest or abdomen. Sometimes you can even pick up signals by watching the shadow of a person's shoulder against a background wall. You can see the pattern of rising and falling with every breath.

Rapid breathing will only mean something about someone's internal state if you've watched them often enough or long enough to know how they breathe when they're excited and when they're calm.

6. Voice Patterns: Tone, Tempo, and Volume

Voices have a number of characteristics, any one of which can vary. The tones can be high or low, loud or soft. The tempo can be fast or slow, with certain pauses or without them. The volume can be smooth or variable, booming or cooing. Some voices squeak, others sing. Again, try not to evaluate what you hear. Notice the range of possibilities and variations in voice among different people and within the same person at different times.

Because there is no visual distraction, telephone conversations offer an excellent opportunity to practice developing your sensitivity to voice changes. To begin, notice just *one* of the dimensions of voice quality: the tone, the volume, or the speed. With practice, you can acquire a sensitivity to all of them.

Influence Scenario 10

The Tell-Tale Signs

Peter, in Wisconsin, always reveals when he's having a
high-pressured day. His voice changes from his usual baritone and
moves up an octave or so. He also increases his volume (as though
his listener were hard of hearing), and he speaks faster. These are
very obvious signals. A perceptive listener would be able to say to
him, "Sounds like you're having a bad day," after he's said only a
sentence or two. He would be amazed at how well even a telephone
acquaintance could "know" him even though the two may have
never met face to face.

Again, don't make assumptions about what changes in voice mean. Simply note the changes. When you've gathered enough examples of how someone's voice alters when they're angry, or how it changes when they are confused, then you can test your assumptions by asking them, "How are you feeling about this idea?"

If you can develop this sensory acuity, you can use your finely tuned radar to notice things that most other people do not. You can be a living lie detector and a powerful influencer.

Representational Systems

Another useful way to refine your listening is to listen for what in NLP theory is called representational systems. This means you must identify which of the five senses — sight, sound, touch, smell, or taste — a person depends upon regularly as a channel through which to perceive the world, process information, and communicate. Some people, for example, experience life as a series of moving or still pictures. Others focus on sounds, such as voices, music, and noise, as a way to "see" the world. They may remember the words they have heard or their own internal voices. Still others experience life primarily through touching and other bodily sensations.

According to proponents of NLP theory, each of us has a preferred sensory channel. If you listen, you will hear people actually *telling* you which one they prefer. They will use certain language and figures of speech which, in effect, tell you something about how their minds work. This is their unique perceptual mode.

A visual person will use phrases like "That's the way I see it," "It seems clear to me," or "Let's watch this carefully."

An auditory person may say, "I hear what you're saying," "That rings a bell," or "It doesn't sound right to me."

A kinesthetic person will use physical or tactile images. His or her language will include expressions like "I'm getting a grasp on the situation," "When the new policy takes hold...," or "It feels right to me."

A gustatory person will use phrases such as "It leaves a good taste in my mouth," "I need to chew on it for a while," or "That's a spicy idea."

Those who trust their noses may say, "It didn't smell right to me," "This deal smells fishy," or "She came out of it smelling like a rose."

By listening for statements like these and learning how to read them, you are on the way to acquiring the fortune teller's craft. It's an important influence skill. Good negotiators make similar judgments consciously *and* unconsciously. And a good poker player masters the control of these nonverbal signals so that his inner state is not revealed to the other players. Of course, most of the people you'll encounter are not ace poker players. They are, however, offering you lots of rich, inside information about themselves. All you have to do is take it.

In Chapter 17 on building rapport, we'll show you how, through entrainment and related techniques, to use the valuable information you can collect as a refined listener to influence others and get the results you want.

16

Refined Listening: Putting It into Practice

Now it's time for you to practice the aspects of listening covered in the previous two chapters, that is, listening for *context*, both external and internal, *content*, and *medium*. Then, you'll be asked to analyze the speech of a fictional boss of yours, and to devise an influence strategy to change his mind.

The Background—Imagine This Scenario

For the last year, you've been in charge of personal computer networks in the management information systems (MIS) division of a mid-sized company. You've designed and installed PC-based local area networks for three groups: the international sales group, the payroll division, and the direct mail marketing group. In all three cases, the PC-based networks replaced antiquated minicomputer systems.

All the new systems share the same basic hardware configurations, so that later on, all PC-based networks that you install can be hooked together. Each division obviously had its own particular computing needs, so each group has a slightly different mix of software.

Your boss is the vice president of the MIS division. You like your boss, although your contact with him has been limited. He's been with the company for a long time, and he is well respected. In fact, he was the one who convinced the company to install the systems you've been replacing. And he hasn't shown any animosity about their being re-placed – quite the opposite. He's let you operate rather autonomously. The few times you've had lengthy conversations with him, he was always positive toward your work. He approved of your performance even more when you sought him out to help you overcome resistance to the first new system you put in.

The last time you had a lengthy discussion with your boss was when you submitted your departmental budget six weeks ago. You kept your re-quests conservative. It was the first budget you had prepared, and it wasn't the time to start asking for new things. You sat together on his office divan as you discussed minor points. He approved it without much dissent.

The Current Situation

Now here's the current situation. Your boss has just sent you a copy of a computer network proposal from the advertising and promotion group in charge of creating the company's catalogs. Their proposal calls for a local area network that is primarily designed for desktop publishing, using graphics, typography, and page-design hardware and software. The prob-lem is that you have an administrative background, not a background in publishing, so you're not too familiar with what the advertising and pro-motion group needs. Your boss, of course, knows this limitation.

Because the advertising and promotion people don't really need numbers or correspondence, they requested a computer system that is much different from the systems you've been installing, and this in-trigues you. You understand that their needs are different, but you also want to examine some alternatives and learn a little more about the needs of a small publishing operation before you recommend a system that may not be compatible with the rest of the systems you've been in-stalling. In your preliminary memo to your boss on the advertising and promotion group's proposal, you indicated your initial excitement about trying something different. You also mentioned that you wanted to do some research to overcome your lack of specific publishing knowl-edge. A day after you send the memo, your boss calls you into his office to discuss the proposal.

To Be or Not to Be

When you go into the office, you see your boss seated behind his desk. He motions you to a chair opposite him on the other side of the desk. You glance around and notice that the divan is covered with paper-work, and his desk is clear except for one folder.

When he sees you, he leans back in his chair and smiles. He engages you in some small talk — about the weather, the local sports scene, and your spouse and kids. He then clears his throat, straightens himself into a more upright position in his chair, opens the only folder on his desk, and looks straight at you.

Of course, you've come to this meeting prepared to take some notes (some clues on the types of questions you should be prepared to ask can be found on the following pages). You're ready to take notes as your boss begins to speak, and this is what he says:

> Let's go over the catalog division proposal. First, I want to make it clear that I really like the work you've been doing. It's important for everyone that the company keep up to date and maintain the competitive edge that these systems give us. But you know that this is just the beginning. I envision that one day the entire company will be wired together, using the most advanced technology.
>
> Now, to the catalog division's proposal. You can see, of course, that their needs are a little different from the other groups for whom you've installed networks. I can also see that you're excited about the possibilities of this new system and the chance to learn a new system. But before you get all excited, let me tell you what I think of this proposal.
>
> You know that they've asked for a different type of system than the ones you've been installing. They say their system will be more versatile and easier to learn, but it's also twice as expensive. Their system can be made compatible with your other networks, but at an even higher cost.
>
> I've looked at the numbers they submitted. The numbers showed a savings, but over a longer period because of the higher cost of the equipment. I'm not sure we have the budget for the initial investment. Here are my thoughts. If we go ahead with this, they'll be totally on their own with this system. No one else in the company will be using it, so they'll be isolated.
>
> My view is that I don't think that we have the capability of supporting this system, even if we install it correctly. I see nothing but support headaches if we accept this proposal. I obviously want your opinion, but I'll tell you straight out that I'm inclined to tell them to forget this idea, and to find a solution that fits in with what we've been doing. The system we design may not be as versatile, but it'll be something we recognize and can deal with. What do you think?

Influence Exercise 29: Using Refined Listening

Your boss is looking at you. He's waiting for your response. Did you write down some questions? Good. Specifically what you plan to ask is not so important at this point as your getting in the habit of phrasing your questions in the way that draws out speakers and facilitates listening. Now, let's go over the refined listening elements discussed in the previous chapter, and see what can be made of your boss's speech. Let's start with the most basic: sorting for influence styles.

Listening for Influence

First, based on your understanding of the six influence styles, which style do you think *you*, the employee, are in this situation? Take a couple of minutes to think about it. If you need to refer to some of the previous chapters, go ahead. Then, write down what style you think you are in the space provided in Exercise 29.

Influence Exercise 29: Using Refined Listening

STYLES

Your Style:_____

Boss's Style:_____

CONTEXT

External

Environment:

_____

Meaning:_____

_____

Internal Context

Relationship:_____

_____

Range:_____

_____

Record:_____

_____

(*Continued*)

Reasons:_____

_____

Rules:_____

_____

Resistance:_____

_____

CONTENT

_____

_____

_____

_____

_____

MEDIUM/SENSORY CHANNEL

Boss's channel:_____

How you know:_____

_____

YOUR WIN/WIN STRATEGY

_____

_____

_____

_____

_____

_____

_____

Your Style

Now, let's talk about the clues planted in your fictional profile that should have led you to your answer. You installed systems in a number of divergent groups—a sales group, an accounting group, and a marketing group. These are all different groups and, therefore, a mix of different types of people. You get along with your boss, and you've even managed to use him as a resource. You're willing to hear what the advertising and promotion group has to say, and you're willing to find out things you don't know in order to find the solution to their problem.

All the characteristics you've shown strongly suggest the Welling style. The fact that you install basically the same things in all departments—a conventional approach—could indicate that you have some Felling in you as well.

The Boss's Style

What style is your boss? Again, put your response in the space provided in Exercise 29. He was able to convince the company to install those first computers, and he didn't seem upset that you've been replacing the systems he originally installed. He also said that he wanted this trend to continue, stating this as an overall vision. At first glance, your boss may seem like a Geller—giving priority to this common goal over his own feelings. However, you admit that you really haven't had much of a chance to talk at length to him. And when you did talk to him at length, it was about things that were already being done.

If you listened closely to your boss's speech, you'll notice that his major reticence was the difference between what the advertising and promotion group wanted and what was already established in the company as a whole. Your boss also spoke heavily about numbers. He acknowledged that the proposed system was good, but too different and too expensive in the short run. This indicates that your boss is primarily a Feller, a preservationist, with a touch of Teller, as many "techies" and number-crunchers are. If you wrote Feller, you're getting the feel for it. If not, write Feller next to what you've written. If you thought he's a Geller or a Weller, that's okay. In some ways, your boss is a little of both, but these are not his *primary* styles.

Listening for Context

External Context

Now let's talk about the three parts of refined listening. The first part is *context*. Consider the *external* context: Where was the meeting? You can go back and reread if you don't remember, although you shouldn't have to. Write down your impressions of the environment in the space in Exercise 29. How do you think this external context is intended to influence you? Are you going to be intimidated? Why? Take a moment to jot down how you think your boss is using the physical environment to influence, in the space marked "meaning."

Remember, the meeting is taking place in your boss's office. All his paperwork is on the divan instead of the desk, which is unusual. This could be a setup to put you in a more structured physical location — there's a desk between you and your boss, which is symbolic of the difference in your professional status: he's the boss; you're the employee. This would indicate that he doesn't necessarily want you to be comfortable, or at least that it's not a concern. He wants you to know that he is the boss and that this is going to be his decision, not a joint one. Otherwise, he would have come to your office — or even made the divan available, instead of making you sit in a subservient position with his desk between you. He said he'd listen to what you had to say, but it was obvious that he'd already made up his mind before calling you in.

Internal Context—The Six Rs Framework

Now, consider the internal context. Let's use the six Rs to see what your boss may really be telling you.

Relationship.   What is your relationship with your boss? Write down your answer in Exercise 29, and whatever notes are appropriate.

Let's hope you wrote the obvious: he's your boss. But, while some people are friendly with their bosses, you should have noted that you aren't that close. This is strictly a business relationship. He leaves you pretty much to yourself, so you really haven't gotten much of a chance to know him. This distance between the two of you works to his advantage.

Range.   The second of the six Rs to consider is range. What is your boss's range, and how will this affect your actions? Take a moment to jot down some notes about your boss's range in Exercise 29.

Your boss seems well-connected, since he not only convinced the company to get computers, but then also convinced upper management to change to newer systems. It looks as if whatever he says will go. You're not going to have much recourse if you can't change his mind.

Record.   The third of the six Rs is record. How has he reacted to you and your ideas in the past? Jot down some notes about his record in Exercise 29.

Well, he's been receptive to you and your ideas, which is good news. But you also haven't really suggested anything radical so far. He will listen to you, since he's listened to you in the past, but you'll have to be careful when you try to convince him to let you give this new system a shot.

Reasons. Now consider reasons, the next of the six Rs. Why is he discussing this proposal with you—especially if it looks as if he's already made up his mind? Stop reading to jot down some notes about reasons in Exercise 29.

He wants your support, even if he has to order you to give it. But also keep in mind that you've pretty much had your own way for the last year. Maybe all the external context is just an act. He certainly seems to have gone out of his way to make it clear he's the boss in this situation. This just may be his way of asserting his authority. If this is just posturing on his part, a compromise that allows him to remain in charge could be worked out.

Rules. What are your boss's rules, the fifth R? What guidelines does your boss use to decide things? Stop to jot down some notes in Exercise 29 on your boss's rules.

Since you suspect that your boss is a Feller, you can assume that he likes things to be orderly. Most of his discussion centered on keeping things orderly, predictable, and by the numbers.

Resistance. In evaluating the internal context, the final R to consider is resistance. How resistant has your boss been to proposals—yours or anyone else's? Jot down some notes on your boss's resistance in Exercise 29.

Your boss seems to have been pretty receptive to your proposals, but he is a Feller, so he'll always have a certain amount of resistance to anything different. As long as you stay within tradition and maintain continuity, you won't have any trouble. But it's obvious that this proposal has shaken him—he isn't sure about a lot of things, which shows resistance.

Listening for Content

Now that you have analyzed the context, think about the content. Think about what has just been discussed about the situation and the observations made. Now, summarize what you think your boss is trying to tell you. Take a moment to jot down some of your thoughts about what your boss is actually saying.

After considering the contextual questions, what your boss is saying is rather simple. He has reservations about the idea. He trusts you, but he wants to assert his authority. As far as one can tell, all the signs indicate that he's willing to discuss it, but he wants you to remember that he is the boss and that it's his final decision.

Without an analysis like this, you might just have accepted your boss's decision not to approve the proposal. Or, more dangerous, you might have gotten into a technical argument on the pros and cons of the new system, which isn't really the main issue. But since you have listened carefully, you can see that he not only is willing to discuss the proposal, but he also has revealed some opportunities for you to influence him and convince him.

Listening for Medium

Now consider the third part of refined listening, namely, the medium, or preferred sensory channel. Since you couldn't see your boss, you obviously can't be expected to identify any physiological changes. You also haven't had enough time to study your boss in this example.

Nonetheless, we all have a preferred sensory channel — how we perceive things. Some clues to your boss's preferred sensory channel were planted in the language he used. Write down what you think his preferred sensory channel is in Exercise 29.

Did you listen carefully enough to pick up these clues? If you listened closely to your boss, you should have noted some key words he used:

"You can *see*, of course..."

"I've *looked* at the numbers..."

"My *view* of this is..."

"The numbers *showed* a savings."

Your boss used *visual* words: *see* and *view* and *look* and *show*. This probably indicates that he is picture-oriented. So, any presentation that you make to him should be visual. You'll need to *show* him how the new system could work.

Creating a Win-Win Situation

Now that you know his style and his preferred sensory channel, how would you try to change his mind? You should have a good idea of what your boss actually wants, how he will react to specific ideas, and how he can be influenced. Write down some ideas in the space provided in Exercise 29.

1. It has been established that your boss is primarily a Feller. So you have to at least plant the idea that the new computer network isn't as radical as he believes.

2. Next, you should stall for time. Because he's a Feller with a touch of Teller, he likes logic, facts, and reasons. Although you're in favor of the new system on principle, you don't have enough information to structure a logical argument. You're pretty sure that his "I'm in charge" act is just that — an act. He just wants to make sure you know that he's the boss.

You should recognize that if you ask him to hold off until you've had a chance to do some research that will satisfy everyone, he'll give you the time. You'd use the answers he gave you to your questions to know exactly what information would satisfy him.

3. Your goal now is to come up with a strategy, a solution that confirms your boss's authority, satisfies his need for conformity, and enables you to work on designing the new network. In other words, a win-win situation.

A Final Note

While doing Exercise 29, you may have felt that the process was very long and involved. That's because you're unfamiliar with it. After you have practiced using various parts of the refined-listening tips, you'll get better and better at analyzing people and situations. You will increase your ability to influence people in a wide range of situations.

17

The Magic of Rapport: Setting the Stage for Greater Influence

Many people think that there is something magical about rapport: "It's kind of hard to explain," they say. "Even when we don't discuss something, I always know just how the other person feels."

Rapport is the feeling of trust and comfort we have when we're with someone who knows, hears, understands, accepts, and values us. Some people call it chemistry. It is usually the result of a close association between two people who have had shared experiences or who share a common philosophy or background. Sometimes rapport comes quickly—often because of shared interests or perhaps because a person reminds you of someone with whom you already have rapport—but usually it takes years to develop.

Rapport is the foundation of most of our relationships. Without it, no matter how much we may like or respect another person, we feel distant, removed, or out of sync with people for whom we may otherwise have high regard or respect. With it, we may disagree or see some things differently, but we still feel that we basically have a connection, an identifiable bond, with someone else—sometimes with people we have very little in common with.

If you have feelings of rapport with a good number of people and get positive feedback from others, you are probably already practicing some of the techniques discussed in this chapter (although you may not be conscious of it).

Fine, you say. You have it with some people, but with others, you just don't; for no matter what you do or say, you can't make a connection with certain people.

Although real rapport, a true meeting of the minds, usually comes when you have a close relationship with someone, there are ways to achieve rapport with another person quickly while you're waiting for a deeper dimension to develop in it. The process involves using the very simple principle of *entrainment* (a process whereby two or more units become synchronized), which is the basis for rapport. If you use entrainment, you'll find that you can establish rapport with almost anyone, even people with whom you never thought you could connect.

Entrainment and the Rhythm of Rapport

In 1665, Dutch scientist Christian Huygens noticed that two pendulum clocks, mounted side by side on a wall, would swing together in precise rhythm. They would hold their mutual beat far beyond their capacity to be matched in mechanical accuracy. It was as if they *wanted* to keep the same time — sort of a mechanical rapport. Huygens assumed a sort of sympathy between the two. From his investigations came the first explanation of what was to be called mutual phase-locking of two oscillators, a scientific way of defining entrainment.

The phenomenon, it turns out, is universal. Whenever two or more oscillators in the same field pulse at *nearly* the same time, they tend to lock in so that they pulse at *exactly* the same time. Why?

Scientists have concluded that nature seeks the most efficient energy state, and it apparently takes less energy to pulse in cooperation than in opposition. It is most economical to have periodic events that are close in frequency occur in phase or in step with each other.

Itzhak Bentov, in his book *Stalking the Wild Pendulum*, described this same phenomenon, which he called *sympathetic resonance*. He recalled an experiment with two tuned violins. One was placed on a table. A violinist played a note on the other one. The same string that was being played was also humming on the violin that was on the table.

Humans also have the capacity for sympathetic resonance. There seems to be some sort of a hold mechanism that takes place between two people in conversation. Dr. William Condon of Boston University's medical school called it the *conversational dance*. He spent a year and a half studying a film of a 4½-second conversational sequence between two people.

He found that listeners were observed to move in precise, shared synchronicity with the speaker's speech. This appears to be a form of entrainment since there is no discernible lag even at 1/48 of a second. It also appears to be a universal characteristic of human communications and perhaps characterizes much of animal behavior in general. By consciously seeking entrainment with someone, you can start a process that leads to instant rapport, which provides the ideal setting for your influence.

Communication is thus like a dance, with everyone engaged in intricate and shared movements across many subtle dimensions, yet all strangely oblivious to what they are doing. Even total strangers display this synchronization. A listener usually does not move as much as a speaker. There are moments when he or she remains quite still. If the listener does move, however, the movements will tend to be synchronous with the speaker's activity. Dr. Condon's conclusion is the more you move in rhythm with someone, the closer you become with that person.

Even when pairs or groups start out aggressively toward one another, a shift in rhythms can sometimes occur. Dr. Paul Byers of Columbia University uncovered an example of this with a tribe in South America known as the Fierce People. When the two village chieftains first encounter each other, they yell and scream and gesture wildly. The two men's pitch and energy levels are very similar. While it looks and sounds like an angry shouting match, the content of what they're saying gradually becomes less important. In the end, they feel less hostile toward one another.

There are many examples of this sort of entrainment, of matching rhythm, all around us.

- A baby's heartbeat synchronizes with that of its mother.
- A powerful public speaker causes the hearts of listeners to beat in rhythm with his.
- Members of an orchestra, all playing different instruments, move, indeed almost breathe, as one.

Dr. Byers has reported that a variety of bodily processes can become synchronized through close interaction.

- Synchronized heartbeats have been reported between psychiatrist and patient.
- Female college roommates sometimes find their menstrual cycles synchronized.
- Physical activities such as singing, rowing, or even marching synchronize the breathing of everyone in the group.

While many may decry small talk as frivolous and urge us to get to the point, small talk often functions as a necessary overture to entrainment.

Entrainment as Rapport

The kind of entrainment just described is like a human law of gravity. Personnel specialist Edgar B. Wycoff noted that with a slight modification Newton's Law would express a human truth: "One person's thoughts are attracted to another person's thoughts with a force directly proportionate to the similarity of their experiences."

When you want to establish rapport with someone, regardless of whether or not you agree with the content of his or her communication, the most expeditious and effective way is consciously to seek entrainment with that person.

You can succeed by first practicing the refined listening discussed earlier. Then match, pace, or mirror one or more of the unconscious rhythms or gestures of the other person. This effort is in keeping with the basic principle of the formula for success: Influence = Attentiveness (refined listening) + Flexibility (altering your habits to match or mirror what you've seen or heard the other person say or do).

As illustrated by the examples in this chapter, matching and pacing your rhythms with those of another person are at the heart of influence. You want to alter your habits to match and pace what you see the other person doing, and echo the voice, tone, and tempo the other person uses. The ability to match the rhythms of someone you want to influence enables you to use the different styles of influence with the best results.

The principles of matching, mirroring, pacing, and leading can be used with *any* aspect of a person's communication. You can begin, for example, with an auditory person by matching the use of auditory language (such as "I hear you..." or "He's in tune with what we're doing...") until you've established rapport. Then, if you want to *show* him your report, he may be more receptive to operating in a visual mode. The important thing is, you've first joined him in his perceptual mode and talked to him in *his* language.

Regardless of the subject matter or form with which you intend to match, mirror, pace, and lead, the principle is always the same: First, join people where they are. Establish rapport. Once you're in tune with them, they're far more likely to respond to you and your efforts to influence them.

Remember, when you are trying to establish instant rapport through entrainment, you must do it in a subtle way so that it's not noticed; otherwise, the people you ultimately want to influence will think (rightly so) that you are mimicking them. What you want to aim for is *approximating* their nonverbal behaviors, so they will sense (on an unconscious level) that you are in harmony with them. And, you, too, will have an internal feeling of "being with" the other person. If, for instance, you sit (or stand, or move) the same way as someone else, you might have a deeper experience of what it is like to be that person, to be feeling his or her feelings, and to have another perspective.

Another important point is that at times it may be appropriate to *break* rapport in order to disengage from a conversation. How do you do this? The easiest way is to *mis*match; that is, when the other person does a particular gesture, instead of matching it, you do something else. One sure way is to look at your watch, or break eye contact, or stand up when the other is sitting. You can also increase your distance from the other person or make an abrupt, unexpected movement.

When seeking rapport through entrainment, it is essential to understand that there is a pattern of physiological (body) changes that a person generally exhibits during the course of a conversation. This pattern can be thought of as the *medium* of another person's communication. In many cases, you simply want to note these changes and build a physiological dossier on each person you want to influence. It is important to recognize that there are other physiological patterns we not only note, but react to. We want to get into rhythm with a person's physiological patterns.

Matching Breathing

As we discussed in the chapter on refined listening, observation is the first step in matching breathing. Begin by noticing the pattern, pace, and rhythm of the other person's breathing. People breathe high in the chest, or low, or deep in the abdomen. While they're speaking, they breathe fast or slow, with or without pauses. You can gauge someone's breathing by observing the rise or fall of the person's shoulders or the pulse points in the neck or chest.

Then check your own breathing and see which elements (speed, rhythm) are the same or different. Try to synchronize or match *one element at a time*. You may notice, for example, that the person is breathing quite slowly. If your breathing pattern is quick, slow it down until it matches the speed of the other person's. Pretty soon you'll be able to match more than one element, and you'll be breathing in sync with the other person. He or she will feel it, too.

Matching Voice

In business, the easiest and most successful matching technique involves voice. You can match the other person's speed or volume or intonation. You must do this with some subtlety, however, or you run the risk that people will think you're mimicking them. And you shouldn't do it with such precision that it sounds foreign and radically different from your own speech pattern. You do not want to parrot; instead, the aim is to approximate one or two aspects of the other person's speech. Be efficient and economical when you do this. Use the least number of moves. A slight adjustment in tone or speed may be all you need to be in sync with someone. Then you don't have to do anything else. The two of you will be in sympathetic resonance. He or she will feel (as you will, often beyond your conscious awareness) that you both are in harmony.

Mirroring Movements and Gestures

Imagine you are meeting an influential client in his office. You want to attain an initial rapport before trying to influence this person. You sit in a chair, and place a folder across your lap. He sits rather stiffly and upright in his desk chair. His hands move constantly, straightening out papers on his desk. Of course, you can't pace his hand movements since you don't have any papers to shift. But you can sit just as stiffly without being in exactly the same position. And you don't want to react immediately; if you do, it will look as if you're mimicking him. As your conversation progresses, work to pace his actions and vocal tone.

In this situation, here's how the pacing and matching would work.

- He leans across the desk toward you.
  You lean slightly toward him.

- He leans back in his chair.
  You lean back to your original position.

- Soon, his hands stop moving around. He folds them in front of him. You, of course, had your hands that way, on top of a folder in your lap. He's now mirroring you! You now have built a good foundation of rapport by speaking the same body language.

But don't expect cues to be immediate as in this example. Entrainment happens over the course of a long conversation, so be observant and patient. Remember, too, that you want to approximate these behaviors, not mimic them. There's a fine line between emulation and mimicry.

For instance, you don't want to match another person's nervous tics, stammers, or accents. You don't want to call attention to what you're trying to do or insult the person you're trying to influence. Anything you do that's too far outside your normal physiological repertoire will be noticeable.

So practice this mirroring in a low-risk situation. Try it with a store clerk or a stranger on a train or plane. The idea is to choose just one or two patterns. Use these patterns to establish instant rapport.

Mirroring with Words

When you have observed and listened to another person and discovered that his or her primary mode of experiencing is, say, visual, then the best way to gain rapport is to speak the same language. Match, as well as you can, your mode of expression to that person's mode. Put your questions in language that appeals to the visual: "Can you *see* yourself owning this?" or "Shall I *show* you how it works?" You can also show visuals—graphs, charts, drawings—to a visual person. Simply telling the person something may not be enough.

Similarly, if someone uses an auditory mode of expression, package your communication with auditory-based language: "How does this *sound* to you?"; "Do you think this idea has the right *tone*?"; or "Will this *ring a bell* with management?"

If it's not readily apparent which form of communication a person prefers, you may have to use the trial-and-error approach. If you don't get a response at first, switch to another mode. If the auditory doesn't work, try the kinesthetic: "How does this *feel* to you?" or "Let's *touch base* so we can get a *firm grasp* on the project."

A common mistake people make is to interpret a lack of meaningful response as resistance when in fact they've simply failed to communicate in a language that really registers in the other person.

Influence Scenario 11

If at First You Don't Succeed...

Recently I was trying to interest the editor of a large magazine in some of our audiocassettes as an educational tool for her readers. I kept telling her about the tapes. I sent them over to her office so she could listen to them. Weeks went by. She asked me if I had a written summary of the tapes.

I told her that since she had the real thing, she could listen to them on her cassette player. Finally, I got the picture. She was a visual person. She'd worked in the magazine world all her life and was more comfortable with something when she saw it rather than heard it. She didn't tell me this; I had to deduce it.

I had my secretary type an entire transcript with a summary and diagrams of the tapes. Two days later, she called and said, "They're great!" She then admitted that she still hadn't listened to the tapes but liked the transcripts well enough to say yes. To my knowledge, she still hasn't ever listened to those tapes. But I got the response I wanted. I established rapport by matching her preferred sensory channel. She *saw* it in print.

This was a great lesson for me. There was nothing wrong with the content of what I presented. The audio form was simply the wrong medium to use in dealing with a visual person.

Influence Scenario 12

Form as Content

Imagine that Bill is having a meeting with a high-level manager of a large corporation. When he enters his office, he notices attractive posters and striking black-and-white photographs on the walls, and many charts and graphs on the bulletin board. They talk for over an hour. Bill notices that his client's conversation is sprinkled with many visual phrases such as *different perspective, the view down the road*, and *getting the big picture*. Recognizing that his sensory mode has a strong visual component, Bill could, in future meetings, match it by using visual aids — slides, charts, and pictures — to help communicate his ideas to the client most effectively. Once Bill gets what he wants — an agreement to support his project — he would appreciate the way the client acknowledges the rapport he feels the two of them have if his parting words were, "We certainly seem to *see eye to eye!*"

Often, what's most important is not so much the content of what you present, but the medium (language) you use to convey it — that is, not *what* you communicate, but *how* you communicate it. Mirroring with words is an important way to establish the instant rapport you need in order to maximize your influence.

Implementing What You've Learned

You should begin implementing this entrainment process slowly, starting in a low-risk situation, such as when a friend stops in to chat or a new supplier pays you a sales visit. Start by pacing just one thing — their breathing, voice, or gestures. See what comes most easily for you. After you've developed some mastery of one skill, then you can try it out in a

higher-risk situation, such as when you're making a sales call. And remember, there are no negative results, no right way or wrong way—it's
an experiment and the world is your laboratory.

Even once you're proficient, you'll probably be in need of an opportunity to establish rapport. This is where small talk comes in. It can be a
valuable tool for establishing rapport on many levels. You can start the
conversation by asking the other person a question or two about himself. (Remember that questions concerning other people's hobbies or interests are always good: their golf game, their new house, their new car.
Keep away from business for the first few minutes, and if the topic
turns to gossip or bad-mouthing, just change the subject to let them
know you are not interested in griping and complaining.)

While they're discussing their golf game or new patio, you should listen only peripherally to the *content* (what the handicap was, how many
pieces of slate went into the patio) and focus on the nonverbal cues. Pick
one or two of these (voice, body posture, gestures, etc.) and *match* and
pace this while you're listening.

Of course, you must also listen to the words, just in case the topic
comes up again later, but your main interest for starters is the nonverbal "story" they're making available to you. After a few minutes of
this very useful small talk, you'll find that you both feel comfortable and
are ready to begin the business discussion. The more you practice this
technique, the more you'll notice the magic of it.

Leading the Way

Establishing rapport, though, is just the beginning. Once in sync, a person is likely to follow you. When this role reversal occurs, you know
you've gained rapport and can start to use that rapport to gain influence. This step is called *leading*.

Rapport Is Just the Beginning

Matching and mirroring usually help you to establish rapport with another person. Once in sync, that person is likely to follow the next step
you take. If you're ready to try influencing them, then your next step is
to lead.

Remember, pacing is simply doing something similar to the other
person in any of the ways discussed here: matching breathing and voice,
mirroring gestures, voice tone, posture, and language style. Leading is
doing something different.

First, you need to evaluate whether or not you've gained the rapport you want. If you have been successful, the other person will follow your lead when *you* do something different from the mirroring gesture. That will be your signal that you've been successfully achieving rapport and that the other person is open to following your lead. You've been told this, however, only in a nonverbal way. You can now send up a trial balloon (in selling, it's called a trial close) to see if the other person seems willing to accept your idea or proposal.

If you notice that the other person is not following your lead, then go back to pacing. This process of matching, pacing, and leading is a continuous one. You may mirror another person's posture for a while and notice if he or she follows your lead when you change position slightly. Then you can continue mirroring and leading.

Influence Scenario 13

Testing by Leading

Remember the influential client whose gestures, movement, and body language Bill was emulating? Bill thought he had achieved a measure of rapport when the client folded his hands as Bill had. Later, Bill tested the client. Here's how he did it: He leaned forward, and, ever so slightly, ran his hand along the rim of the folder in his lap. After a short while, the client sits up. Then, the client began to move his hand across the top of his desk. Quite unconsciously, he was seeking to establish rapport with Bill. At the end of a discussion with all this following and leading going on, Bill heard the compliment, "I had a good feeling about you—it feels as if we're in sync about this project."

In Sum

People in general will be far more likely to respond to your influence when you work with good rapport. Remember that Attentiveness + Flexibility is the principal secret of influence. Therefore, you must be attentive to all their idiosyncratic behaviors, from the way they breathe to the way they influence, and you must watch and mirror these behaviors in a natural, subtle way. Your flexibility enables you to take the lead.

Beyond entrainment, rapport involves matching influence styles. If the other person is a Teller, use logic. If she's a Compeller, make her feel as if she's in charge. If he's a Weller, supplement his skills. If she's a Feller, establish continuity with the past. If she's a Seller, get small concessions. If he's a Geller, establish a long-range vision. This process results in the rapport that sets the stage for your influence.

By establishing good rapport on a variety of levels and speaking the same language, you're employing all seven secrets of influence. Once in sync — in tune — with the people you want to influence, you're in the best possible position to get them to respond favorably to your ideas and thus to achieve your goal.

Epilogue

In this book you have learned to identify and understand the business environment of the coming decade and how it will affect you. You've studied the important workplace issues, conditions, and challenges that make the need for influence so vital.

You've learned the basic definition of influence and examined some of the myths and misconceptions about it. You know what influence is, and what it's not.

You've discovered the six-style theory of influence (six of the secrets) and the specific skills and behaviors of each style.

You learned the most important principle for successful influencing—the seventh secret: Influence = Attentiveness + Flexibility.

You did practice exercises for each of the six styles to further develop your sharpness and "radar." You developed your attentiveness by learning how to recognize each style, and you developed more flexibility in your own repertoire.

You discovered the many different aspects and subtleties of listening, in refined listening—such as the context, the content, and the medium of a communication; the six Rs of any relationship; passive listening; active listening; listening for representational systems; nonverbal listening; and the power of precision.

You now understand the magic of rapport and its important principles of matching and pacing in every human communication. You learned to make conscious and strategic that which has been unconscious and random. You are now a much more elegant and artful communicator.

Now you're a more tuned-in listener, a more aware and awake communicator, a more strategic influencer. You're in charge now, with attentiveness, flexibility, and influence making a more powerful you.

Good luck. And much success in your life and work. If you keep practicing these few simple ideas on a daily basis, you certainly will enhance your chances to fulfill your every dream and goal.

Appendix

Characteristics of and Findings from the Influence Styles Inventory

The Influence Styles of Male and Female Managerial and Nonmanagerial Staff in Major U.S. Corporations: Results from Studies Utilizing the Influence Styles Inventory

The data presented and analyzed in this appendix are part of Success Strategies' ongoing studies of influence styles originated in the 1980s.

The data analyzed were obtained from the Success Strategies Influence Styles Inventory (ISI), a unique questionnaire instrument created and developed by Success Strategies especially to distinguish two types of information: (1) the relative strength of each type of influence style possessed by individuals and (2) the relative strength of each type of influence style for different categories of individuals, such as men and women and managers and nonmanagers within corporations.

Characteristics of the Success Strategies Influence Styles Inventory (ISI)

Items and Procedure.   The ISI is a forced-choice instrument containing 55 pairs of statements. For each pair, individuals are asked to select the choice they believe most accurately describes how they behave in work situations when they have the need to influence or persuade others. For example, item 1 on the ISI presents the following choices: (*a*) "I recognize that reward is a strong motivator" and (*b*) "I try to present my ideas appealing to logic rather than emotion"; for item 6 on the ISI, respondents are asked to select one of the following choices: (*a*) "I let people know up front what is required of them" and (*b*) "I'm satisfied when people agree to only a piece of what I'm proposing."

Scoring the ISI. Using item 6 on the ISI, just described, to illustrate the scoring procedure, next to choice *a* is the number 2 and next to choice *b* is the number 5. These numbers, which run from 1 through 6 on the ISI, each represent a different influence style. For example, number 2 represents the Compelling influence style and number 5 represents the Selling influence style. All six of the influence styles are described in Table A-1.

The maximum ISI score an individual can attain for a given influence style is 19. The scores an individual receives for each of the six influence styles show which influence style is most characteristic of the individual, next most characteristic, and so on, down to least characteristic. The six influence style scores define the influence style profile for each individual, group of employees, or corporation.

Table A-1. Types of Influence Styles and Scoring Codes

Influence style	Scoring code	Characteristic feature
Telling/Analyst	1	Attempts to influence by reason, logic, evidence, data
Compelling/Pragmatist	2	Attempts to influence by bargaining, negotiating, invoking higher authority, rewards, and punishment
Felling/Preservationist	3	Attempts to influence by winning over others, pointing out flaws
Welling/Catalyst	4	Attempts to influence others by listening, gaining rapport, joining
Selling/Strategist	5	Attempts to influence others by presenting ideas in benefits, targeting to others' needs and goals
Gelling/Idealist	6	Attempts to influence by creating and joining common visions and dreams

The Types of Influence Styles and Their Scoring Codes

Table A-1 presents each type of influence style, the ISI scoring code assigned to it, and a brief description of its major characteristic.

Example of a Success Strategies ISI Profile. Based on the above scoring procedure, an individual might have an ISI profile as follows: 1 = 16, 2 = 12, 3 = 11, 4 = 2, 5 = 9, 6 = 5. The total of the six scores adds up to 55, the number of items on the ISI.

This frequency distribution of scores tells us that the individual has a predominantly Telling/Analyst style, because influence style number 1 occurred most often (16 times). This means that the individual mainly attempts to influence through reason, logic, evidence, and data. In contrast, this individual least attempts to influence through the Welling/Catalyst style (influence style number 4), i.e., by listening, gaining rapport, and joining. In addition, we can see that this individual has a weak Gelling/Idealist influence style (number 6), and thus is unlikely to try to influence based on creating and joining people in common visions and dreams.

In between these extremes, we can see that this individual is about equally likely to exhibit the Compelling/Pragmatist style (number 2), Felling/Preservationist style (number 3), and Selling/Strategist style (number 5)—all of which suggest reliance on, among other things, reasoning and ideas (consistent with this person's dominant influence style, Telling). In this example, we also can see that these three characteristics are relatively typical of the individual, with scores of 12, 11, and 9, respectively.

In this manner, those who administer the ISI to workers (or others, such as clients) can profile individuals in the workplace as well as compare different categories of workers, such as men and women and managers and nonmanagers.

Reliability of the ISI. Statistical tests of significance, by Dr. William Vingiano of New York University, have determined that the ISI is a reliable research instrument. To determine reliability, the six influence styles dimensions were tested using the split-half correlation technique. All correlations were significant at the .05 level, ranging from .619 to .915.

In addition, two overall dimensions of the scale were subjected to a test of reliability: Dimension A, consisting of the Telling, Compelling, and Felling influence styles (representing the "Autocratic" influence orientation, characterized by basically "left-brain" mental functions), and Dimension D, consisting of the Welling, Selling, and Gelling influence styles (representing the "Democratic" influence orientation, char-

Table A-2. Means and Standard Deviations for Influence Styles, by Sex (Men = 28, Women = 46) and Employment Status (Managers = 47, Nonmanagers = 27) at L'Oreal

Influence style	Totals		Male		Female		Managerial		Nonmanagerial	
	$\bar{X}$	SD	$\bar{X}$	SD	$\bar{X}$	SD	$\bar{X}$	SD	$\bar{X}$	SD
Telling	10.66	3.66	11.50	3.23	10.40	3.59	11.00	3.38	10.22	3.42
Compelling	10.97	2.48	10.78	2.83	10.79	2.21	10.70	3.30	11.30	2.25
Felling	4.58	2.73	5.07	3.11	4.28	2.46	5.17	2.93	3.56	2.02
Welling	9.75	3.53	10.04	4.11	9.64	3.84	9.53	3.50	10.25	3.86
Selling	10.16	2.91	9.57	2.57	10.49	3.11	10.11	3.02	10.30	2.80
Gelling	8.19	3.66	7.64	3.53	8.52	3.73	8.21	3.80	8.15	3.46
Autocratic	8.73	2.95	9.12	3.06	8.49	2.75	8.75	3.21	8.36	2.62
Democratic	9.37	3.37	9.08	3.40	9.55	3.56	9.28	3.44	9.57	3.37

Table A-3. Means and Standard Deviations for Influence Styles, by Sex (Men = 35, Women = 13) and Employment Status (Managers = 31, Nonmanagers = 17) at MCI

Influence style	Totals		Male		Female		Managerial		Nonmanagerial	
	$\bar{X}$	SD	$\bar{X}$	SD	$\bar{X}$	SD	$\bar{X}$	SD	$\bar{X}$	SD
Telling	12.33	3.59	13.06	3.87	11.60	3.22	12.07	3.14	10.23	2.31
Compelling	7.62	3.58	10.50	4.37	9.75	3.18	11.45	4.03	8.80	1.97
Felling	7.24	3.51	11.88	3.56	6.84	2.97	7.16	3.62	7.33	3.00
Welling	10.55	4.93	11.37	3.01	9.70	4.44	9.50	3.78	11.59	2.75
Selling	8.12	3.89	7.51	4.05	8.74	3.36	7.82	3.12	8.42	3.65
Gelling	7.42	2.42	5.99	2.85	8.86	3.03	8.64	3.34	6.20	2.86
Autocratic	9.06	3.22	11.81	3.84	9.40	3.71	10.23	4.35	8.79	2.35
Democratic	8.70	2.37	8.97	2.11	9.10	2.09	8.65	3.52	8.74	2.71

acterized by basically "right-brain" mental functions). The correlation of .875 was significant at the .01 level, supporting the reliability of the Autocratic/Democratic dimensions of the ISI.

Findings from Studies of Major U.S. Corporations

Throughout the 1980s and into the 1990s, the ISI has been administered to male and female managerial and nonmanagerial staff at a variety of major corporations, including L'Oreal, MCI, IBM, Banker's Trust, American Express, Bellcore, the Learning Annex, WDRG, and AT&T. The various studies conducted by Success Strategies have supported each other regarding the distribution of influence styles between the sexes and levels of workers, but differences also have been noted.

The most recent studies conducted by Success Strategies have been at L'Oreal and MCI during the latter part of 1990. Findings from these studies are shown in Table A-2 (L'Oreal) and Table A-3 (MCI). The tables compare the arithmetic means (averages) and standard deviations for each of the six influence styles and the Autocratic/Democratic scales, broken down by, respectively, the sex of the subjects and their managerial status.

By comparing the statistics for Tables A-2 and A-3, we can note the differences and similarities in the influence style profiles at L'Oreal and MCI, including distinctions between the men and women and managerial and nonmanagerial personnel within each company and between the companies. For example, considering all personnel for the two companies, at L'Oreal the dominant influence style was Compelling (mean = 10.97), whereas at MCI the Compelling style was among the least characteristic (mean = 7.62) and the Telling style (mean = 12.33) was dominant. (At L'Oreal the Telling style was the second most characteristic, only slightly behind the Compelling style.)

Table A-4 shows the rank ordering of the six influence styles at L'Oreal and MCI, with 1 indicating most characteristic and 6 indicating least characteristic.

As Table A-4 shows, the greatest disparity between the two companies existed for the Compelling style, with Welling indicating the next greatest disparity. For the other influence styles, the companies were remarkably similar.

However, comparisons based on simple rankings, such as are presented in Table A-4, can conceal significant facts about companies. For example, although Felling was the least characteristic influence style at both L'Oreal and MCI, when one looks at the means for Felling for the two companies, one can see that this influence style was much more

Table A-4. Rank Ordering of Influence Styles at L'Oreal and MCI

Influence style	L'Oreal rank	MCI rank
Telling	2	1
Compelling	1	4
Felling	6	6
Welling	4	2
Selling	3	3
Gelling	5	5

dominant at MCI, with a mean of 7.24, than at L'Oreal, with a mean of 4.58. Further, regarding the Felling style, it may be noted that it was similar for men (mean = 5.07) and women (mean = 4.28) at L'Oreal but that there was a wide discrepancy in this style between men (mean = 11.88) and women (mean = 6.84) at MCI.

According to this analysis by sex, in fact, we can see that the Felling style was pronounced among men at MCI (second only to the Telling style for men), a fact obscured by the mean score for all personnel (which was lowered by the relatively weak display of this orientation among the women). Further regarding the Felling orientation at MCI, in contrast to the strong sexual difference, there was almost no difference between managers (mean = 7.16) and nonmanagers (mean = 7.33) with respect to this influence style. At L'Oreal, on the other hand, there was a rather strong difference involving Felling between managers (mean = 5.17) and nonmanagers (mean = 3.56).

Aside from showing distinctions for the individual influence styles, Tables A-2 and A-3 reveal an important distinction between the companies for the composite dimensions, Autocratic and Democratic. For all personnel, at L'Oreal the Democratic orientation (mean = 9.37) was greater than the Autocratic orientation (mean = 8.73), whereas at MCI the Autocratic orientation (mean = 9.06) was greater than the Democratic orientation (mean = 8.70).

Given this difference, one wonders, "Is a 'left-brain' orientation (Autocratic) more functional for a company like MCI and a 'right-brain' orientation (Democratic) more functional for a company like L'Oreal?" If so, what is it about the internal structure of these companies, their products and services, or their customers that necessitates this difference in influence style orientation? Or is it that the difference in influence style orientation between the companies is merely an artifact of the particular personnel employed at the time of the study? Research providing answers about the appropriateness of the influence style orientation of company personnel would be of value to any company interested in creating harmony among the key aspects of its operation, for the sake of maximum efficiency, productivity, worker morale, and profitability.

The analysis and discussion just presented are not meant to be exhaustive, of course, but rather suggestive of the kinds of information and insights that can be gained, and questions that can be raised from scrutinizing research findings produced by the Success Strategies Influence Style Inventory.

To further enable you to see the kinds of similarities and differences between companies and categories of personnel within companies that are revealed by the ISI, we now present findings from a recent large, representative study involving the personnel at seven major U.S. corporations: IBM, Banker's Trust, American Express, Bellcore, the Learning Annex, WDRG, and AT&T (including two separate divisions, designated AT&T1 and AT&T2).

Table A-5 presents data for the personnel of the seven companies considered collectively, and shows the arithmetic means (averages) and standard deviations for each of the six influence styles and the Autocratic/Democratic scales, broken down by, respectively, the sex of the subjects and their managerial status.

As Table A-5 shows in the Totals column, the most prevalent influence style was Telling (mean = 11.03), virtually tied by Welling (mean = 10.73). The least prevalent influence style was Gelling (mean = 7.19) with the Compelling (mean = 9.02), Selling (mean = 8.29), and Felling (mean = 8.09) influence styles between the high and low extremes. The difference between the Telling and Gelling influence styles was about 4 points, or roughly one-fifth of the maximum possible range any two values could achieve.

As regards the index measures, the Autocratic influence style (composed of the Telling, Compelling, and Felling styles) was slightly more prevalent than the Democratic influence style (composed of the Welling, Selling, and Gelling styles) with means of 9.38 and 8.74, respectively.

When these data are looked at in terms of the sex of the subjects, an almost identical picture emerges. For men the most prevalent influence style was Welling (mean = 11.12), virtually tied with Telling (mean = 10.97); for women, again these two influence styles were virtually tied, but their order of magnitude was reversed, with the Telling style (mean = 11.07) slightly ahead of the Welling style (mean = 10.45). For both sexes, Gelling also was the least prevalent influence style.

A rather sharp difference existed between the sexes, however, for the index measures. Whereas for the men there was only a .34 difference between the Autocratic (mean = 9.24) and the Democratic (mean = 8.90) influence styles, for the women there was a .87 difference — more than 2.5 times greater than for the men — with the Autocratic style showing a mean of 9.49 and the Democratic a mean of 8.62.

Table A-5. Means and Standard Deviations for the Influence Styles Exhibited by the Personnel at IBM, Banker's Trust, American Express, Bellcore, the Learning Annex, WDRG, and AT&T, by Sex (Men = 120, Women = 148) and Employment Status (Managers = 138, Nonmanagers = 115)

Influence style	Totals		Male		Female		Managerial		Nonmanagerial	
	$\bar{X}$	SD	$\bar{X}$	SD	$\bar{X}$	SD	$\bar{X}$	SD	$\bar{X}$	SD
Telling	11.03	3.98	10.97	4.05	11.07	3.94	10.46	4.01	11.73	3.74
Compelling	9.02	3.04	8.41	2.90	9.50	3.08	9.02	3.12	8.97	2.89
Felling	8.09	3.90	8.33	4.18	7.91	3.67	7.78	3.76	8.31	4.08
Welling	10.73	3.81	11.12	4.00	10.45	3.63	10.45	3.74	10.96	3.89
Selling	8.29	3.37	8.44	3.51	8.18	3.27	8.47	3.60	8.10	3.16
Gelling	7.19	3.42	7.13	3.31	7.22	3.53	7.65	3.30	6.81	3.50
Autocratic	9.38	3.81	9.24	3.11	9.49	2.57	9.09	7.21	9.67	3.23
Democratic	8.74	2.20	8.90	3.61	8.62	2.85	8.86	6.74	8.62	2.58

It will be noted, however, that for both sexes the Autocratic style was more common than the Democratic style.

When the data in Table A-5 are looked at in terms of the managerial status of the subjects, again the same picture emerges. For managers and nonmanagers alike, the Telling influence style was the most prevalent, virtually tied with Welling style, and the least prevalent influence style for both groups was the Gelling style. Specifically, for managers, the Telling mean was 10.46, the Welling mean was 10.45, and the Gelling mean was 7.65; for nonmanagers, the Telling mean was 11.73, the Welling mean was 10.96, and the Gelling mean was 6.81.

Also for these groups, the Autocratic style was more prevalent than the Democratic style: for managers, the Autocratic mean was 9.09 and the Democratic mean was 8.86, representing only a .23 difference; for nonmanagers, the Autocratic mean was 9.67 and the Democratic mean was 8.62, representing a 1.05 difference—nearly 5 times greater than the difference for the managers.

Thus, in regard to the index scores, whereas for men and managers there was a very slight difference between Autocratic and Democratic influence styles, for women and nonmanagers there was a much greater difference between these styles. This indicates a sharper difference between "left-brain" (Autocratic style) and "right-brain" (Democratic style) orientations among women and nonmanagers than among men and managers. It may be noted that this finding contradicted what one would expect, given that, for example, women are stereotypically held to be more "intuitive" (right-brained) than men. Whereas the difference between these modes was greater for women and nonmanagers, it should be remembered, however, that members of all groups exhibited a stronger tendency towards the Autocratic than the Democratic influence style orientations.

The Statistical Significance of the Differences in Influence Styles between Groups: Analysis of Variance (ANOVA)

For the data in Table A-5, we also determined which of the observed differences were statistically significant, i.e., unlikely to have occurred by chance. In addition, we were interested in determining if the influence styles were significantly related to the combination of the subjects' sex and work status, e.g., if there was an *interaction effect* between being male and a nonmanager or between being female and being a manager. To answer these questions, the analysis of variance, or ANOVA, tech-

Table A-6. Means and Standard Deviations for Influence Styles, by Corporation

Influence style	Bellcore (n = 82) X	SD	IBM (n = 36) X	SD	Learning Annex (n = 12) X	SD	Banker's Trust (n = 15) X	SD	American Express (n = 20) X	SD	AT&T1 (n = 41) X	SD	AT&T2 (n = 31) X	SD	WDRG (n = 31) X	SD
Telling	11.28	3.58	12.47	3.75	9.67	4.42	10.73	4.04	12.05	3.00	9.81	4.98	10.45	4.03	10.90	3.71
Compelling	8.59	3.20	9.50	2.95	10.58	3.00	7.67	2.13	10.05	2.44	8.39	3.19	9.19	2.95	9.52	2.95
Felling	8.38	4.07	7.19	3.81	8.67	4.21	6.27	4.32	7.00	3.16	7.81	3.90	9.84	3.38	8.45	3.68
Welling	10.94	4.07	10.78	3.56	8.92	3.48	10.93	4.50	10.55	3.27	10.10	3.88	11.77	3.71	10.61	3.56
Selling	8.37	3.14	7.89	3.35	7.92	4.10	9.60	4.10	8.10	2.94	8.54	3.64	8.13	3.78	8.07	3.03
Gelling	7.16	3.26	7.11	3.45	8.33	2.61	7.90	3.42	7.40	3.00	7.98	3.84	5.39	3.36	7.23	3.52
Autocratic	9.42	3.28	9.72	3.19	9.64	3.80	8.22	3.22	9.70	3.12	8.67	3.52	9.83	3.15	9.62	3.07
Democratic	8.82	2.77	8.59	2.49	8.39	2.86	9.47	3.46	8.68	2.59	8.87	3.15	8.43	2.48	8.63	2.42

nique was employed, with findings considered statistically significant at the .05 alpha level or less.

The results of the ANOVA showed that there were statistically significant differences between managers and nonmanagers for the Telling style, Gelling style, and Autocratic orientation; a statistically significant difference between men and women for the Compelling style; and a statistically significant interaction effect for sex and managerial status in explaining variation in the Welling influence style.

Specifically, for the Telling style, managers had a mean of 10.46 and nonmanagers had a mean of 11.73; for the Gelling style, managers had a mean of 7.65 and nonmanagers had a mean of 6.81; and for the Autocratic orientation, managers had a mean of 27.76 and nonmanagers had a mean of 29.02. In regard to the statistically significant difference between men and women for the Compelling influence style, men had a mean of 8.41 and women had a mean of 9.50. For the significant interaction effect between sex and work status in explaining variation in the Welling influence style, male nonmanagers had a mean of 11.38, male managers had a mean of 10.72, female nonmanagers had a mean of 9.93, and female managers had a mean of 11.22. As can be seen from these data, the biggest difference existed between male and female nonmanagers, which was only slightly greater than the difference between female managers and nonmanagers.

In addition to analyzing the influence styles in terms of the sex and managerial status of the workers at the corporations, the influence styles also were analyzed for all personnel in each of the corporations analyzed in Table A-5, irrespective of their sex and managerial status. The results of this analysis are shown in Table A-6.

Findings for Differences in Influence Styles by Corporation

To more easily see the main trends in influence styles by corporation, Table A-7 presents, for each influence style, the corporation with the highest mean.

As can be seen from Table A-7, five of the eight corporations studied are represented, with AT&T2 being represented three times and Banker's Trust and the Learning Annex each being represented twice. The three corporations not represented in the table are American Express, AT&T1, and WDRG. It should be emphasized, however, that for each of the influence styles, there was a relatively slight difference between the majority of the corporations.

Table A-7 also clearly shows that, with rare exception, none of the influence styles was very strongly represented in any of the corpora-

Table A-7. The Dominant Influence Style at Each Corporation

Influence style	Corporation	Mean
Telling	IBM	12.47
Compelling	Learning Annex	10.58
Felling	AT&T2	9.84
Welling	AT&T2	11.77
Selling	Banker's Trust	9.60
Gelling	Learning Annex	8.33
Autocratic	AT&T2	9.83
Democratic	Banker's Trust	9.47

tions, given that the maximum score for an influence style is 19. The highest mean for any of the individual influence styles, shown in Table A-7, was 12.47 for the Telling style at IBM. The lowest mean was 8.33 for the Gelling style at the Learning Annex. These results, regarding the relative frequency of the influence styles in the individual corporations, are consistent with the findings reported earlier in this appendix for the subjects looked at collectively, irrespective of corporation, and in terms of their sex and managerial status.

When the data for L'Oreal and MCI (Tables A-2 and A-3), presented earlier, are considered along with the data in Table A-7, a slightly different picture emerges, with L'Oreal holding the highest scores for two influence styles, Compelling and Selling. These data are shown in Table A-8.

With respect to the Autocratic and Democratic dimensions for the nine corporations discussed in the appendix, several interesting differences and similarities may be noted. From Table A-7, it can be seen that the highest Autocratic orientation, at AT&T2 (mean = 9.83), and the highest Democratic orientation, at Banker's Trust (mean = 9.47), were separated by only a .36 difference. Within certain of the corporations, however, there was a marked difference in the Autocratic and Demo-

Table A-8. The Dominant Influence Style at Each Corporation

Influence style	Corporation	Mean
Telling	IBM	12.47
Compelling	L'Oreal	10.97
Felling	AT&T2	9.84
Welling	AT&T2	11.77
Selling	L'Oreal	10.16
Gelling	Learning Annex	8.33
Autocratic	AT&T2	9.83
Democratic	Banker's Trust	9.47

cratic orientations. For example, at IBM, the Autocratic mean was 9.72 and the Democratic mean was 8.59, a difference of 1.13. A similar difference was exhibited at AT&T2, where the Autocratic mean was 9.83 and the Democratic mean was 8.43, a 1.4 point difference in favor of the Autocratic orientation. In contrast, a more Democratic orientation was evident at Banker's Trust, where the Democratic mean was 9.47 and the Autocratic mean was 8.22, a 1.2 point difference. In still other corporations, the Autocratic and Democratic orientations were nearly identical. For example, at AT&T1, the Democratic mean was 8.87 and the Autocratic mean was 8.67, a .20 difference; and at MCI, the Autocratic mean was 9.06 and the Democratic mean was 8.70, a .36 difference.

These findings and the others discussed throughout the appendix show that the personnel at the major corporations in America have distinctly different influence style profiles and this fact, in turn, produces consequences for the corporations, as discussed or implied throughout this book.

Index

About the Author

Elaina Zuker is president of Success Strategies, Inc., a management training and consulting firm in New York and San Francisco. She has provided consulting services to many of the nation's most prestigious organizations, including AT&T, American Express, Dun & Bradstreet, IBM, the Sheraton Corporation, and other *Fortune* 500 comapnies. The author of *The Assertive Manager* and of Day-Timer "Success Enhancement" Series audiocassette programs, she is a speaker much sought after by businesses, associations, and conferences.